Quiknotes

Devotional
Classics

Here are some other useful books
in the *Quiknotes* series.
Add them to your library of
quick-reference books, today:

Quiknotes: The Books of the Bible
Quiknotes: The Books of the New Testament
Quiknotes: The Books of the Old Testament
Quiknotes: The Origin of the Bible
Quiknotes: English Bible Versions
Quiknotes: Christian History
Quiknotes: Christian Classics
Quiknotes: Great Women of Faith

Quiknotes™
DEVOTIONAL CLASSICS

Daniel Partner

Tyndale House Publishers, Inc.
WHEATON, ILLINOIS

Visit Tyndale's exciting Web site at www.tyndale.com

Copyright © 2000 by Daniel Partner. All rights reserved.

Cover illustration copyright © 1996 by Cathie Bleck. All rights reserved.

Much of the biographical information in the summaries has been adapted from *Who's Who in Christian History* (Wheaton, Ill.: Tyndale House Publishers, Inc.).

Quiknotes and the Quiknotes logo are trademarks of Tyndale House Publishers, Inc.

Edited by David Barrett

Unless otherwise indicated, all Scripture quotations are taken from the *Holy Bible,* New Living Translation, copyright © 1996. Used by permission of Tyndale House Publishers, Inc., Wheaton, Illinois 60189. All rights reserved.

Scripture quotations marked KJV are taken from the *Holy Bible,* King James Version.

Scripture quotations marked RSV are taken from the *Holy Bible,* Revised Standard Version, copyright © 1946, 1952, 1971 by the Division of Christian Education of the National Council of the Churches of Christ in the United States of America, and are used by permission. All rights reserved.

Scripture verses marked TJB are taken from *The Jerusalem Bible,* copyright © 1966, 1967 and 1968 by Darton, Longman, & Todd, Ltd., and Doubleday & Company, Inc.

Library of Congress Cataloging-in-Publication Data

Devotional classics / Daniel Partner.
    p. cm. — (Quiknotes)
  ISBN 0-8423-3333-9 (pbk.)
  1. Devotional literature—Abstracts. I. Partner, Daniel. II. Quiknotes (Wheaton, Ill.)
BV4801.D387 2000
248—dc21   99-042243

Printed in the United States of America

06 05 04 03 02 01 00
7   6   5   4   3   2   1

CONTENTS

INTRODUCTION

The ideal Christian life rotates around an axis of two poles: One is action, the other, devotion. A Christian is active in service to the church and the world and is also singularly devoted to God. While church history clearly records the believers' actions, one must search church literature to learn of their devotion. This collection of summaries is intended to help readers begin studying and enjoying Christian devotional literature.

Please note that this collection is far from complete. Many books eloquently express personal longing for Christ, the search for true spirituality, and love for God. A comprehensive collection of these books would far exceed the limits of this small work. A book that a reader may have personally enjoyed or considered significant in this genre might not be found in this collection for various reasons. Rather than an exhaustive survey of Christian devotional literature, this book is simply an introduction to certain well-known titles and to other important (though lesser-known) works, with the hope that the reader will be inspired to read the works themselves.

The titles summarized here are drawn from the many eras of church history and have withstood the test of time. They are generally recognized as significant Christian literature. They are also still in print or are commonly available through libraries. The articles herein are presented in chronological order of publication. In addition to summarizing a work of devotional literature, each includes biographical and historical information important to the understanding of the author and the concerns and emphases of the work.

The Middle Ages

.... *Confessions* **c. 410**

Augustine of Hippo (354–430)

Augustine was born of a pagan father and a Christian mother in the North African town of Tagaste. His parents recognized that their son was gifted and sought for him the best Roman education. He eventually studied rhetoric at Carthage, where he abandoned the faith of his mother, adopted an intemperate lifestyle, and took a mistress by whom he fathered a child.

But Augustine was also stirred to a religious quest for wisdom through philosophy. For nine years Augustine followed the Manichaeans, who saw the world as a grand interplay between two equally powerful forces—absolute good and absolute evil. To them the God of the Old Testament was the evil power, and the God of Christianity was the power of good.

Eventually, Augustine found problems with this philosophy that he could not resolve. In the meantime, he moved to Rome to start a school of rhetoric. There he searched the writings of the Skeptics, who believed true knowledge cannot be obtained. He also attended the preaching of the Christian bishop Ambrose in order to hear his eloquence. Ambrose's allegorical preaching presented answers to the questions Augustine had raised with the Manichaeans. When Augustine was appointed professor of rhetoric in Milan in 384, he found Christian intellectuals there who instructed him in the faith. In time he read the New Testament book of Romans and came to understand Christ as a moral authority over him. This, said Augustine, gave him a "new will."

Augustine's sudden moral conversion caused him to leave teaching in order to pursue truth. He was baptized by Ambrose on Easter of 387, and in 388 returned to North Africa after the death of his mother.

At that time the North African church was struggling with the heretical influence of the Manichaeans and the Donatists. When visiting Hippo, Augustine was convinced by the believers there to be their priest. In 396 he became bishop of Hippo, where he would remain until his death.

The barbarians plundered Rome in 410. Pagans blamed the fall of the city on the Christians who had deserted the old Roman gods. Christians were caught in a bind—they had claimed that God would protect the empire of the Christian emperors. Refugees who reached North Africa demanded an answer from Augustine. He answered through his work *City of God,* a systematic, biblical view of history and the state.

By the year 430 Roman North Africa had been destroyed by the barbarians along with much of Latin Christianity. As Hippo was held in military siege, Augustine ministered to a congregation swelling with refugees, and he even melted the church's gold vessels to provide for them. Soon after this, Augustine contracted a fatal disease and died.

Confessions is the best known of Augustine's writings. This introspective autobiography provides a clear picture of a life under the transforming power of the Christian gospel. It is an emotionally moving book that testifies of Christ's work in this great man. In summary of the book Augustine wrote:

> My *Confessions,* in thirteen books, praise the righteous and good God as they speak either of my evil or good, and they are meant to excite men's minds and affections toward him. At least as far as I am concerned, this is what they did for me when they were being written and they still do this when read. What some people think of them is their own affair; but I do know that they have given pleasure to many of my brethren and still do so. The first through the tenth books were written about myself; the other three about Holy Scripture.

The first section of *Confessions* (Books 1–10) moves from Augustine's birth to his rebirth with a "new will" in Christ and ends with the death of his mother, Monica. After his conversion, Augustine tried to understand all of God's creation with his new will. So the second section of *Confessions* (Books 11–13) is an examination of the inner world and the outer world, with a perceptive study of memory and time.

Confessions describes Augustine's self-examination as a Christian and reflects a clear biblical understanding of human nature and the fallen condition. Augustine elevates the grace of the gospel and finds God's grace acting in his own life.

Concerning the devotional quality of *Confessions,* Augustine himself wrote in his *Letter to Darius* (429):

> Thus, my son, take the books of my *Confessions* and use them as a good man should—not superficially, but as a Christian in Christian charity. Here see me as I am and do not praise me for more than I am. Here believe nothing else about me than my own testimony. Here observe what I have been in myself and through myself. And if something in me pleases you, here praise Him with me—Him whom

I desire to be praised on my account and not myself. "For it is he that hath made us and not we ourselves." Indeed, we were ourselves quite lost; but he who made us, remade us. As, then, you find me in these pages, pray for me that I shall not fail but that I may go on to be perfected. Pray for me, my son, pray for me!

In *Confessions*, Augustine addressed himself eloquently and passionately to the enduring spiritual questions that have stirred the minds and hearts of thoughtful people since time began. As a result, *Confessions* constitutes perhaps the most moving diary ever recorded of a soul's journey to grace.

◆ Augustine of Hippo, *The Confessions of Saint Augustine.* New York: Doubleday, 1972.

. . . . *Rule of St. Benedict* **c. 540**
Benedict of Nursia (c. 480–c. 547)

Benedict was born in Nursia, a small town in the middle of Italy. While pursuing his education in rhetoric and law at Rome, Benedict became repulsed by the immorality he found there. He left Rome before finishing his studies and went to live in a cave near Subiaco. Eventually Benedict became the abbot for a group of monks near the area. After a short while, however, he was asked to leave because the monks there resented his strictness. Returning a second time, Benedict was again forced to leave because of a jealous priest. Around 520 he established a monastery at Monte Cassino, where he stayed until his death. It was here that Benedict drew up his *Rule.*

The *Rule of St. Benedict* is composed of a prologue and seventy-three chapters. Benedict compiled and modified his *Rule* from a variety of earlier rules and practices of other monastic communities. Through simple, direct language,

Benedict expanded on these earlier rules, augmenting them with his own understanding derived from experience. He devised a balanced and flexible system for bringing order to monastic communities and giving meaning to everyday life experiences. According to Benedict, if order and meaning could be established, the higher attributes of wisdom and virtue could also be attained.

Benedict's *Rule* can be considered a monastic directory of operations that is both spiritual and practical. The *Rule* addresses primarily daily activities and concerns of the monastery: meals, work, clothing, travel, worship, etc. It prescribes a balance of prayer, work, and study and calls for strict adherence to poverty, chastity, and obedience. The *Rule* is characterized by moderation, sensibility, and humanity. Benedict believed that such common concerns, rightly accomplished, could lead to perfection. Benedict was opposed to the extreme ascetic practices of some monks. Instead, he sought to create an environment where believers could pursue the service of God and their own spiritual improvement through a balanced life of manual labor, reading, prayer, and worship.

According to the *Rule*, a monk's relationship with God is mirrored in his relationship with the abbot of the monastery as well as with the other monks of the community. Those called to the monastic life share all things in common, forgive offenses, and live in compassion for others' weaknesses. Allowances are made in the *Rule* for individual differences, such as age, capability, disposition, needs, spiritual maturity, and weaknesses. The broad and simple spirituality of the *Rule* makes it adaptable to various local traditions.

Overall, the *Rule* challenges the individual to become empty of self-interest and self-will and to live in trust of God's mercy rather than in anxious fear. Such emptiness and trust are characteristics of the perfect life of love. Here is a brief excerpt:

The Lord seeking his workman in the multitude of the people, to whom he proclaims these words, says again: "Who is the man that desires life and loves to see good days?" [see 1 Peter 3:10]. If hearing this you answer, "I am he," God says to you: "If you will have true and everlasting life, keep your tongue from evil, and your lips from speaking guile; turn away from evil and do good; seek after peace and pursue it" [see Psalm 34:12-14]. And when you shall have done these things, my eyes shall be upon you, and my ears unto your prayers. And before you shall call upon me I will say: "Behold, I am here." [Language updated.]

Although there is no evidence that Benedict originally intended to found an entire order of monks, he did intend for his *Rule* to be followed in monasteries all over Europe and Asia. Benedict's hopes for a broad range of readership can be seen in the considerations he makes for certain rules, such as the allowances he makes for clothing styles because of differences in climate.

The legacies of Benedict's *Rule* are numerous. These included the practice of a one-year probation for new members; the lifetime election of the abbot; and the function of officials, such as prior, steward, novice master, guest master, etc. Benedict forbade the ownership of even the smallest item and ordained that silence should prevail in the monastery. Monastic bodies have drawn upon the spiritual treasury of the *Rule of St. Benedict* for centuries, and other institutions have benefited from its wisdom as well.

The endurance of the *Rule* over the centuries is testimony to the devotional value to the church of its wisdom and insight.

◆ Benedict of Nursia, *The Rule of St. Benedict*. Translated by Anthony C. Meisel and M. L. del Mastro. New York: Doubleday & Co., 1975.

.... *The Little Flowers of St. Francis*
Francis of Assisi (1182–1226)

Francis was born in 1182, the son of Pietro Bernardone, a
wealthy cloth merchant, and his wife, Giovanna di Pica. Francis
worked with his father until he embarked on a military adventure at age twenty. Imprisoned for many months as a result, he
reflected on his life. By 1204 he had become quite disenchanted
with his reckless youth and materialistic values.

Two events profoundly changed the life of Francis. The first
was a pilgrimage to Rome, where he knelt to give alms to a
leper and kiss his sores. The second was a revelation he received
in a little ruined church called San Damiano on the outskirts of
Assisi. There, a voice from the crucifix said to him, "Francis,
repair my falling house." He took the words literally and sold a
bale of silk from his father's warehouse to pay for repairs to the
church of San Damiano. His father was outraged and thought his
son insane. There was a public confrontation at which his father
disinherited and disowned Francis, who in turn renounced his
father's wealth.

Declaring himself "wedded to Lady Poverty," Francis abandoned all material possessions and devoted himself to serving
the poor. Since he could not pay for repairs to the church of San
Damiano, he undertook to repair it by his own labors. He lived
with the priest of the church, begged for stones lying useless
in fields, and used them in repairing the church. He got his
meals not at the expense of others but by scrounging crusts and
discarded vegetables from trash bins and by working as a day
laborer, insisting on being paid in bread, milk, eggs, or vegetables rather than in money.

Francis did not intend to establish a religious order, nor did
he anticipate disciples. But soon a diverse group of companions
joined him. These people included Bernard of Quintravale, a

wealthy merchant; Sylvester, a cleric; Giles of Assisi, a devout peasant; and Juniper, a slightly mad mystic.

In addition, Francis helped the sixteen-year-old Clare leave her wealthy family to become the first of an order of mendicant sisters. ("Mendicant" refers to those who own nothing and survive by begging alms.) In his *Canticle of Brother Sun,* Francis tells how he and his early disciples musically expressed their faith and communion with God through nature. After another vision, in the chapel of Porziuncola in 1208, the Friars Minor began their mission of preaching repentance, singing, aiding the peasants in their work, and caring for lepers. In his first-known letter to all Christians, Francis wrote:

> O how happy and blessed are those who love the Lord and do as the Lord himself said in the gospel: "You shall love the Lord your God with your whole heart and your whole soul, and your neighbor as yourself." Therefore, let us love God and adore him with pure heart and mind. This is his particular desire when he says: True worshipers adore the Father in spirit and truth. For all who adore him must do so in the spirit of truth. Let us also direct to him our praises and prayers, saying: "Our Father, who art in heaven," since we must always pray and never grow slack.

In 1210 the pope authorized the forming of the Order of Friars Minor, commonly called the Franciscans. (*Friar* means "brother," as in fraternity, and *minor* means "lesser" or "younger." These monks were younger brothers of Christ.)

The heart of Francis's message was poverty. To renounce wealth was to find true freedom to serve God and the needy. The "first rule" issued in 1221 stated: "The friars are to appropriate nothing for themselves, neither a house, nor a place, nor anything else. . . . They beg alms trustingly." Francis and his companions took the words spoken by Jesus Christ literally when he sent his disciples out to preach:

> Preach as you go, saying, "The Kingdom of Heaven is at hand." . . . You have received the gospel without payment, give it to others as freely. Take no gold, or silver, or copper in your belts, no bag for your journey, no spare garment, nor sandals, nor staff [see Matthew 10:7-10].

Their task was to preach, "using words if necessary," declaring by word and action the love of God in Christ.

The Lateran Council of 1215 attempted to curb the friars' "excessive enthusiasm" and reorganize the brotherhood under existing monastic rules. But Francis's friendship with the powerful cardinal Ugolino (later Pope Gregory IX) saved the order from dissolution and won the right to subsist by begging.

Francis lacked administrative skill, so Ugolino increasingly dominated the order's policies, while Francis occupied himself with missionary work and spiritual guidance. Eventually the order suffered from its own success. Many people were attracted by Francis and his air of joy, abandonment, and freedom. What many overlooked is that these were made possible by his willingness to accept total poverty—not picturesque poverty, but real dirt, rags, cold, and hunger. When there were only a few friars, they were all known to Francis personally, and the force of his personality kept the original ideals of the order alive in them. As the order grew, this was no longer possible.

In 1220 Francis resigned as minister-general of the order, and in 1221 he agreed to a new and modified rule, which he did not approve but could not reject. When the direction of the order passed beyond his control, Francis retired to a semihermetic life. After extended illnesses he died on October 4, 1226.

The spirited and beloved Italian classic, *The Little Flowers of St. Francis of Assisi* (*Fioretti di Santo Francesco d'Ascesi*), was first published in 1476. It is a collection of tales about St. Francis and his earliest disciples. But, contrary to folklore, these stories have a certain authority as history.

After the death of Francis, his secretary and friend, Leo (who is quoted extensively in *The Little Flowers*), lived until 1271. Giovanni dalla Penna, one of the early missionaries of the order in Germany and another one of the sources, did not die until 1274. But by 1257 two conceptions of Francis himself were current in the order. His biography was being recounted in different ways. Eventually, Bonaventura wrote the "official" biography. He made it more official still by burning all conflicting accounts.

Perhaps as early as 1250, no later than 1261, a monk known as Ugolino of Montegiorgio began writing *Floretum*, or "garden of flowers." To him the term *flowers* meant *notabilia*, "more noteworthy things." These were things omitted from the formal biographies of Francis. But the older members of the order knew that the omission of these facts distorted and misrepresented the spirit of the early days of Francis and the Order of Friars Minor.

The earliest known manuscripts of the present book date from 1390 as an anthology of Franciscan miracles. The *Floretum* of Ugolino did not extend beyond the year 1261; however, the manuscript dealt with episodes occurring in 1322. Apparently its compiler knew Ugolino personally and so probably utilized other writings of Ugolino.

The standard Italian edition by Antonio Cesari was published in Verona in 1822. The first English translation of *The Little Flowers of St. Francis of Assisi* (*Fioretti di Santo Francesco d'Ascesi*), by Lady Georgina Fullerton, appeared in 1864. The first American translation, by Abby Langdon Alger, was published in 1887. The present century has witnessed numerous other translations in England and America, with dozens of editions in America alone.

The American translation of *Little Flowers* by Alger runs fifty-three short chapters. The first bears this subtitle:

> In this book are contained certain little flowers, miracles, and devout examples of that glorious poor follower of Christ, Saint Francis, and of certain of his holy companions. Told to the praise of Jesus Christ.

The Little Flowers of St. Francis is a simple Italian masterpiece of folk art. It recounts the early period of Franciscanism much as it was lived by the friends and disciples of Saint Francis. Its method is to present concepts as suggestive images: Saint Francis's nibbling at his loaf of bread in order not to sin by equaling the Lord's fast of forty days; the pope's curiosity at seeing Clare make the cross appear in the crust of her bread; the friars' dialogues with their translated brethren; the saint wrestling with the devil; Satan's revenge—a landslide with the swish of his tail; the astonishment of the ladies and the cavaliers at the holy spectacle of the first chapter; etc.—all scenes that could be depicted in medieval paintings. All these pictures might have been painted with the humor and bright pallet of the American folk artist Grandma Moses had she been a thirteenth-century Franciscan.

As the book proceeds, the images multiply, and it deepens in devotional beauty. Chapter 8 is subtitled *How Saint Francis and Brother Leo, as they journeyed, discoursed of perfect bliss.* It ends with these words of Francis to Leo:

> And yet hearken unto the end, Brother Leo. Beyond all the graces and gifts of the Holy Ghost, which Christ has granted unto his faithful friends, is victory over self, and power for love of Christ to suffer pain and insult, poverty and disgrace; forasmuch as in all the other gifts of God we can take no pride, they being not our own but of God. Hence the Apostle saith, "What have ye which is not of

God? And if it be of him, wherefore do ye glory in it, as
if ye had it of your own selves?" But in the cross of sorrow
and grief we may glory, inasmuch as the Apostle saith,
"God forbid that I should glory, save in the cross of Christ."

◆ Ugolino et. al. *The Little Flowers of Saint Francis of Assisi.*
New York: Vintage Books, 1998.

. . . . *The Dialogue of Catherine of Siena*
Catherine of Siena (1347–1380)

Catherine du Giacomo di Benincasa was born among the
youngest of twenty-five children to a wealthy dyer of Siena in
present Spain. It is said that at the age of six she had a vision of
Christ in glory, surrounded by his saints, and that from that time
on, she spent most of her time in prayer and meditation. What
is known is that at the age of sixteen she joined the third order
of St. Dominic. As a Dominican lay sister she led a strict ascetic
life in her own home. Later she became a nurse and led an active
public life of menial service, ecclesiastical reform, and political
diplomacy.

Catherine of Siena was a mystic—a contemplative who
devoted herself to prayer; a humanitarian—a nurse who worked
to relieve the suffering of the poor and the sick; an activist—a
renovator of church and society who did not hesitate to speak
truth to power; and an adviser and counselor—who made time for
the problems of troubled and uncertain souls. She acquired a reputation for insight and sound judgment, and many persons from
all walks of life sought her spiritual advice. Although she was
almost illiterate, Catherine influenced many through her dictated
letters. In Siena she exercised great authority over her followers.

Catherine's era was one of chaos for the church and society.

In 1376 she visited Pope Gregory XI, who was in exile in Avignon, France. She hoped to persuade him to return to Rome. The popes, officially bishops of Rome, had been living in Avignon for about seventy years. There they were under the political control of the king of France. Eventually Pope Gregory XI did return to Rome. Catherine then acted as his ambassador to Florence in an attempt to reconcile a quarrel between the pope and the leaders of that city.

After Gregory's death in 1378, the cardinals elected the Italian pope Urban VI. He turned out to be arrogant, abrasive, and tyrannical. So the dissatisfied cardinals met again and elected another pope, Clement VII, who established his residence at Avignon. Catherine labored to persuade Urban to reform; her letters to him are respectful but uncompromising. She also promoted the idea that the peace and unity of the church required the recognition of Urban as lawful pope. But, despite Catherine's efforts, the papal schism continued until 1417. This weakened the prestige of the bishops of Rome and helped pave the way for the Protestant Reformation.

Catherine of Siena ranks high among the mystics of the Roman Catholic church. She was canonized in 1461 and declared the patron saint of Italy in 1939. Her book, *The Dialogue,* is her spiritual testament. It begins:

> A soul rises up, restless with tremendous desire for God's honor and the salvation of souls. She has for some time exercised herself in virtue and has become accustomed to dwelling in the cell of self-knowledge in order to know better God's goodness toward her, since upon knowledge follows love. And loving, she seeks to pursue truth and clothes herself in it.

The Dialogue is Catherine of Siena's gift of her teaching to her followers. It is not new theologically. In fact, its author was engaged fully in the main current of the Catholic teaching of her day. Although untrained in theology, she is faultless in her orthodoxy yet fresh and vivid in her expression of the tradition. The book, a dialogue between a soul and God, was not organized by chapters or sections by it's author. Her disciples divided it into chapters and later it was further divided into larger sections. The modern scholar Giuliana Cavallini restored what is thought to be the original structure of the work. There is a regular flow of petition, response, and thanksgiving found in an outline of ten sections: "Prologue"—the fundamental argument of the book; "The Way of Perfection"—various divine instructions; "Dialogue"—a request for three things: mercy for the people of God, mercy for the world, and grace; "The Bridge"—the fourth and central section of the book, a complex metaphor of a bridge to describe the way of truth; "Tears"—an explanation of five kinds of tears, which correspond to the stages of the soul; "Truth"—an explanation of, among other things, three lights that give sight: the imperfect, the perfect, and the most perfect; "The Mystic Body of Holy Church"—a description of the priesthood, eucharistic mystery, evil clerics, and other matters; "Divine Providence"—a description of providence in creation, redemption, the sacraments, the gift of hope, and the law; "Obedience"—an explanation of the Word as remedy to the sin of Adam; and finally, "Conclusion"—a summary of the whole book.

The writing of Catherine of Siena is that of a highly intelligent, spiritual, and devout medieval nun. The reader must remember that she had not passed through the Reformation. *The Dialogue* overflows with allegory, is layered with symbol, and joins a variety of metaphor in an attempt to describe things that flout description. It is no light reading. But it is the crowning work of a significant servant of God and is still accessible to the reader who will take the time to taste and absorb its many flavors.

Here is a sample of Catherine's writing, taken from the section entitled "The Bridge":

> This bridge has walls of stone so that travelers will not
> be hindered when it rains. Do you know what stones
> these are? They are the stones of true solid virtue. These
> stones were not, however, built into walls before my
> Son's passion. So no one could get to the final destination
> even though they walked along the pathway of virtue.
> For heaven had not yet been unlocked with the key of
> my Son's blood, and the rain of justice kept anyone from
> crossing over. . . . I have told you that he is the bridge, he
> built them into walls, tempering the mortar with his own
> blood. That is, his blood was mixed into the mortar of his
> divinity with the strong heat of burning love.

◆ Catherine of Siena. *Catherine of Siena: The Dialogue.* Edited by Suzanne Noffke. New York: Paulist Press, 1988.

. . . . *Revelations of Divine Love* 1393
Julian of Norwich (c. 1342–c. 1413)

Almost nothing factual is known about Julian, but tradition associates her with Saint Julian's church, Norwich, England, which is near the place where Julian lived a solitary life of prayer and meditation. She is also know by many as Mother Julian or Lady Julian.

In May of 1373, when Julian was about thirty years old, she became sick and seemed to be near death for six days. On the seventh day, fifteen revelations, or "showings," began that lasted nearly twelve hours. The next day she received the final vision: Her soul appeared to her as a city, an endless world, and a blessed kingdom with Christ sitting in it.

Julian mediated on these visions for twenty years, concentrating on the love of God, which supplies the answer to all of life's problems and to the evil in the world. Eventually Julian recorded her visions and her meditations on them in the first English literary work written by a woman: *Revelations of Divine Love.*

The times of Julian of Norwich were devastated by the Hundred Years' War, the Black Death, and social and religious upheaval. Against this background, this unlikely author produced a lucid work of Christian mysticism. In *Revelations* she writes:

> In this life there is within us who are to be saved a surprising mixture of good and bad. We have our risen Lord; we have the wretchedness and mischief done by Adam's fall and death. Kept secure by Christ, we are assured, by his touch of grace, of salvation; broken by Adam's fall, and in many ways by our own sins and sorrows, we are so darkened and blinded that we can hardly find any comfort. But in our heart we abide in God, and confidently trust to his mercy and grace—and this is his working in us.

Julian tells that as a young woman she prayed that she would (1) have the knowledge of Christ's suffering; (2) experience serious sickness in order to know the suffering of dying without actually entering death; and (3) receive three wounds: that of true repentance, of kind compassion, and of longing for God. Through sickness and her visions, Julian realized the fulfillment of her desires. The first twelve visions focus on Christ's crucifixion. The pain of these visions was nearly impossible for Julian to endure, but she refused the temptation to look away. Through her visions, Julian came to believe that in our present life believers are "on [Christ's] cross dying with him in our pains and our passion."

Julian's questions about sin and pain were answered by Christ in her visions. She learned that God sends suffering to his children not because they have offended him but to prepare their souls for greater bliss. True to the best of Christian mysticism, *Revelations of Divine Love* maintains a tension between the pain and sin of human life and the love and bliss of the divine. Julian summarized her doctrine of God in this way: "I saw full surely that ere God made us he loved us; which love was never slacked nor ever shall be. And in this love he hath done all his works and in this love he hath made all this profitable to us and in this love our life is everlasting."

Julian mentions the "motherhood" of Christ in her *Revelations*. She was not the first with this concept. Other writers, including Anselm of Canterbury, had previously written of Christ's "motherhood." Julian was the first to list it among the three roles of God: father, mother, and lord. For Julian, God is a father because Christians have their being from him; he is a mother in the mercy he shows; and he is the Lord in the grace he gives.

Revelations of Divine Love (also titled *Showings*) expresses Julian's meditations with conviction, intelligence, and beauty. It has been called "the most perfect fruit of later medieval mysticism in England." And so it has remained a favorite source for mystical contemplation for Christians throughout the ages.

♦ Julian of Norwich, *Julian of Norwich Showings*. Translated by Edmund Colledge and James Walsh. Classics of Western Spirituality series. New York: Paulist Press, 1978.

.... *The Imitation of Christ* **1418**
Thomas à Kempis (1380–1471)

The life and work of Thomas à Kempis are the best known examples of the religious renewal brought about by the Brethren of the Common Life. Thomas Hemerken was born in Kempen (hence his more familiar name "à Kempis") near Cologne in the Rhine valley and studied at the cathedral school at Deventer in the Yssel valley in what is now the Netherlands. While there Thomas met Florentius Radewijns, a highly respected member of the Catholic lay community Brethren of the Common Life.

As was usual for members of this order, Radewijns helped support Thomas in his studies. Thomas also seems to have lived with other Brethren in Deventer. He was ordained a priest in the Canons Regular of Saint Augustine in about 1413 and lived in the monastery at Mount Saint Agnes. By the time he died, his name had made the monastery well known.

Thomas copied many manuscripts, a primary activity of the Brethren. He wrote devotional works, sermons, and chronicles. Many of his works address the topics of poverty, humility, and chastity. There are sermons to novices and a number of biographies of saints. But the principal work for which Thomas is known is the classic devotional *The Imitation of Christ.*

There is great controversy as to the true author of this book. For the most part, contemporary scholars are confident that before his early death in 1374, Gerard Groote wrote the text of *Imitation.* Thomas à Kempis is given credit as its author, but it is more likely that he served as its editor and publisher.

A Dutch scholar of Deventer, Groote was the founder of the Brethren of the Common Life. In 1372 Groote's scholarly life was interrupted by severe illness, and when he recovered, he began to pursue a life of living by the Spirit. He preached a "modern devotion" based on inner spirituality and charitable service. This led to the founding of the Brethren.

When banned from preaching publicly, Groote left Deventer and founded an order of Augustinian canons (communities of priests) in Windesheim. The scholar Desiderius Erasmus, known for his seminal *Greek New Testament*, studied at Windesheim. Groote kept a diary titled *The Following of Christ.* Scholars believe that this is the same work that is attributed to Thomas à Kempis—*The Imitation of Christ.*

This is a manual of spiritual advice to help believers follow Christ's example. The book contains four parts. The first two sections contain general counsel for the spiritual life. The third section explores the inner life of the soul, and the fourth addresses the sacrament of Holy Communion.

The Imitation of Christ teaches that in order to fully understand the words of Christ, the Christian must strive to conform to the life of Christ. This requires the believer to follow Christ in the way of the Cross as well. In other words, the believer must be content with suffering and hardship, "for only the servants of the cross can find the way of blessedness and of true light." Once a believer begins this journey, there is no turning back. The cause of shame in a Christian is the failure to pursue this goal of imitating Christ.

The importance of listening to the gentle voice of the Holy Spirit is emphasized. The inner voice is vital to anyone seeking to imitate Christ. It is dramatically contrasted with the speaking of the prophets of the Old Testament: "Let not Moses speak unto me, nor any of the prophets, but rather do thou speak, O Lord God, the inspirer and enlightener of all the Prophets," says *Imitation*. In order to hear this voice, the believer should also develop a disciplined habit of prayer and meditation.

Humanity is entirely incapable of progressing by its own merit in the holiness described in *The Imitation of Christ:* "There is no worse enemy, nor one more troublesome to the soul, than thou art to thyself, if thou be not in harmony with the Spirit."

The book is somber and demanding, and some say that it is second only to the Bible in its impact on the church. Be that as it may, the six-hundred-year-old insights of *The Imitation of Christ* still inspire devotion to God.

♦ Thomas à Kempis. *The Imitation of Christ.* Translated by William Creasy. Notre Dame, Ind.: Ave Maria, 1989.

The Renaissance
and Reformation

. . . . *The Way of Perfection* **1565**
Teresa of Ávila (1515–1582)

A Spanish mystic and the founder of a reformed Carmelite order, the Discalced (barefoot) Carmelites, the woman now known as Teresa of Ávila called herself Teresa of Jesus. She became a nun at sixteen, but even the relaxed life of the community in which she lived was too restrictive for her, and she suffered emotionally and physically. Yet, little by little she sought new depths of contemplation and at age forty experienced a trance in which for the first time she had a vision of Christ. This she called her "second conversion." Her visions continued and included visions of Christ piercing her heart with a spear.

Teresa's growing spiritual sensitivity caused increasing dissatisfaction with the relaxed ways of her order. Her spiritual accomplishment and discontent led Teresa to dispute with local authorities and those of her order. Thus she resolved to found a reformed order. This was accomplished, against protests, in 1562. Later, John of the Cross worked with her in this effort.

From the new convent of St. Joseph in Ávila, Teresa, a semi-invalid, traveled incessantly throughout Spain, founding and administering seventeen convents, all obedient to the original strict Carmelite rule. This rule emphasized strict enclosure, discipline, and mental prayer. She was a model of rigorous discipline, wearing a hair shirt and often scourging herself.

Teresa was a very practical-minded person with a genuine genius for administration. Yet her literary legacy is her books on the mystical way: *Autobiography* (1562), *The Way of Perfection* (1565), *Book of Foundations,* and *Interior Castle* (1577). These brought her the title Doctor (i.e., teacher) of the Church. Her saintliness and miracles that were reported to have been done by her led to her canonization in 1622.

The Way of Perfection is the most easily understood of all Teresa's writings. Written during the height of controversy that raged over the reforms Teresa enacted within the Carmelite Order, *The Way of Perfection* was composed at the express command of Teresa's superiors and was written during hours that did not interfere with her day's crowded schedule. This classic on the practice of prayer is still fresh—a work of mystical beauty. With simple instructions, exhortations, and inspiration, it composes a practical guide to prayer for people seeking a more perfect Christian life.

"I shall speak of nothing of which I have no experience," Teresa wrote in the prologue, "either in my own life or in observation of others, or which the Lord has not taught me in prayer." The author teaches a deep and lasting love of prayer—the most effective means to attain virtue.

Teresa's first three chapters are a description of the reason for her founding the first Reformed Carmelite convent: the desire to minimize the effects of Protestantism and to check the so-called freedom that was permeating the order. She applauds the virtues of humility and poverty and entreats her readers to practice it in their own lives.

Chapters 4–15 stress the importance of a strict observance of the order's rule and constitution and explain the three essential elements of a prayer-filled life. These are mutual love, detachment from created things, and true humility. For Teresa, the latter of these is the most important and includes the others. Humility is nothing less than truth that gives the precise estimate of one's own worth.

Chapters 16–26 develop these ideas and lead to the themes of prayer and contemplation. Here is found Teresa's famous extended simile of the game of chess, in which the soul gives check and mate to the King of love, Jesus. This section covers questions that may not be of great interest to a modern reader: Can a soul in grave sin enjoy supernatural contemplation? Can all souls attain to contemplation? Is it possible, without experiencing contemplation, to reach the summit of Christian perfection? Have all the servants of God who have been canonized (declared saints) by the church necessarily been contemplatives? Does the church ever grant noncontemplatives beatification? Do contemplatives know suffering?

But chapters 27–42 are concerned with a timeless topic—the Lord's Prayer. For today's reader, here is the heart of the book. These chapters comment on the Lord's Prayer petition by petition. Teresa touches the themes of recollection, quietness, and union; the temptations to which spiritual people are exposed when they lack humility and discretion; mistaken scrupulousness and timidity leading to doubt and despair; spiritual favors; and others.

Finally, Teresa writes of the love and fear of God and prays for her readers. She asks God to protect them from ills and peril until they reach the next world, where all will be peace and joy in Jesus Christ.

The Way of Perfection is a skillful, classic teaching on the rudimentary principles of the spiritual life, and it touches the most sublime and elusive tenets of mystical theology.

◆ Teresa of Avila. *The Way of Perfection.* Translated by Allison E. Peers. New York: Doubleday & Co., 1991.

.... *Dark Night of the Soul* 1578
John of the Cross (1542–1591)

John of the Cross is one of the acknowledged masters of mystical theology. Together with Teresa of Ávila, he founded the Discalced (barefoot) Carmelites, an order devoted to prayer and penance.

Born Juan de Yepes y Álvarez in Fontiveros, Spain, in 1542, John was the son of a wealthy silk merchant, Gonzalo de Yepes, and a poor weaver, Catalina Álvarez. John's father was disowned for marrying beneath his station, and the couple lived in hardship, practicing the trade of silk weaving. John was the youngest of three sons. Shortly after his birth, his father died, and thereafter his mother struggled to provide for her children.

John attended a school for poor children in Medina del Campo and gained a basic education and skills from local craftsmen. At seventeen, he began work at the Plague Hospital de la Concepcion and was allowed to attend the Jesuit College. From 1559 to 1563, John studied with the Jesuits, learning Latin, Greek, and other subjects.

At age twenty, he entered the Carmelite order (1563). John continued his studies at the University of Salamanca and was ordained in 1567. Soon he met Teresa of Ávila, and she encouraged him to promote her reform among the men's order. So in 1568, John and three other friars took up the observance of the primitive Carmelite rule in a farmhouse near Duruelo. At that time, he took the name John of the Cross.

Meanwhile Teresa was ordered to return to the Convent of the Incarnation as its superior. She called upon John to assist her in renewing the large community. In 1572 John became the spiritual director of the nuns, including Teresa herself. But the attitude of the Carmelites began to change toward the reformers, and they ordered Teresa to choose one monastery as her permanent residence.

John was arrested and imprisoned in a windowless six-by-ten-foot room in a monastery in Toledo. Scourged and humiliated, he refused to renounce his reforms and in his cell composed the lyric poems that form the basis of his mystical writing. Months passed, and he managed to escape to the south of Spain, where he had been elected prior of the monastery at El Calvario and appointed director of the nuns at Beas. In 1579, he became rector of the new Discalced Carmelite college near the University of Baeza.

During these years, John wrote the commentaries on his poems illumining the mystical life. Toward the end of his life, he disagreed with some changes in the order and was sent to the solitude of La Penuela (1591). John fell ill after a month at La Penuela. Urged to seek medical attention, he went to the monastery at Ubeda. There he died at age forty-nine.

Dark Night of the Soul is a continuation of the author's *Ascent of Mount Carmel*. This latter work is composed of three sections. First it concerns the sensual part of the soul; second, the spiritual part; third, the activity of the soul. *Dark Night* is the fourth part in this series. The first three tell of a night of the soul, a cleansing of sense and spirit. The fourth concerns passive purification and "is a more obscure and dark and terrible purgation." John explains further:

> God perceives the imperfections within us, and because of his love for us, urges us to grow up. His love is not content

to leave us in our weakness, and for this reason he takes us into a dark night. He weans us from all of the pleasures by giving us dry times and inward darkness.

In doing so he is able to take away all these vices and create virtues within us. Through the dark night pride becomes humility, greed becomes simplicity, wrath becomes contentment, luxury becomes peace, gluttony becomes moderation, envy becomes joy, and sloth becomes strength. No soul will ever grow deep in the spiritual life unless God works passively in that soul by means of the dark night.

In *Dark Night of the Soul,* John of the Cross explains with surprising freshness the purpose of this purging, purifying work: union with God through love. The author is able to infuse philosophy into his mystical commentary with true humanity—even in his loftiest passages. He finds agreement between the natural and the supernatural, between reason and grace, and shows that this Divine grace does not destroy nature, but rather enobles and dignifies it.

◆ John of the Cross. *Dark Night of the Soul.* Translated by Allison E. Peers. New York: Doubleday & Co., 1990.

. . . . *The Sermons of John Donne*
John Donne (1572–1631)

John Donne was born in London to a Roman Catholic family. At the time anti-Catholic feeling in England was high and Catholics were constantly harassed by Elizabethan secret police. Donne nevertheless entered Oxford at age eleven, later studied at Cambridge, and then studied law at Lincoln's Inn, London. He never received a degree and never formally practiced law.

In 1593 Donne's younger brother Henry died in prison after

being arrested for harboring a priest. Donne then abandoned Roman Catholicism and joined the Anglican church. During this period Donne wrote his first book of poems, *Satires.* The manuscript received a fairly wide readership, even though it was only circulated privately. It is considered one of Donne's most important literary efforts. His love poems, *Songs and Sonnets,* were written around this time as well.

In 1596 Donne joined the naval expedition against Cádiz, Spain, led by Robert Devereux, the second earl of Essex. In 1598 Donne became secretary to Thomas Egerton, the lord chancellor, but his prospects for worldly success were dashed when, in 1601, he eloped with Egerton's seventeen-year-old niece, Ann More. Sir George More had Donne imprisoned and dismissed from his post. Poverty and failure followed. Donne later summed up the experience in this way: "John Donne, Ann Donne, Undone." The couple found refuge with Ann's cousin in Pyrford, Surrey, while Donne made a meager living as a private lawyer.

In 1607 Donne refused to take Anglican orders. But King James declared that Donne could receive no employment from him except in the church. In 1615 Donne accepted the king's invitation and entered the Anglican ministry and was appointed royal chaplain. Eventually he was appointed reader in divinity at Lincoln's Inn.

Ann Donne died in 1617 at age thirty-three after giving birth to their twelfth child. In 1621 James I appointed Donne dean of Saint Paul's Cathedral, a position he held until his death. Most certainly Donne would have become a bishop, but his poor health prevented this.

Donne is considered the greatest of the seventeenth-century metaphysical poets, a group that includes George Herbert, Henry Vaughan, and Richard Crashaw. Donne's early poetry, represented best in his *Songs and Sonnets* and *Elegies,* is remarkable for its vivid language, startling and often exaggerated imagery, and frequent use of paradox. The *Divine Poems* of Donne's later years reveal an intensity of feeling and depth of insight rarely equaled in English poetry. Here are four lines from his poem "Good Friday, 1613. Riding Westward," describing Christ's death:

> *There I should see a sun, by rising, set,*
> *And by that setting endless day beget:*
> *But that Christ on this Cross did rise and fall,*
> *Sin had eternally benighted all.*

Donne's private devotions, *Devotions Upon Emergent Occasions* (1624) were written while he was convalescing from a serious illness. "Meditation 17" records his thoughts upon hearing a tolling bell. It contains the well-known phrases, "No man is an island entire of itself" and "Send not to know for whom the bell tolls: it tolls for thee."

Donne was also a great preacher in an age of great preaching. Donne's metaphorical style, learnedness, and wit were seen in his brilliant sermons, full of fervor. Examples of this can be found in his final sermon:

> There we leave you in that blessed dependency, to hang upon him that hangs upon the cross, there bathe in his tears, there suck at his wounds, and lie down in peace in his grave, till he vouchsafe you a resurrection, and an ascension into that kingdom which he hath prepared for you with the inestimable price of his incorruptible blood. Amen.

In addition to his considerable intellectual, spiritual, and rhetorical strengths, John Donne lived a full life for forty-two years before he entered the ministry. He was not merely a student of divinity. Experience with Elizabethan religious and political intrigue, naval expeditions, the corridors of imperial power, romance, elopement, disgrace, poverty, and hack writing all stepped into the pulpit in John Donne. Regarding Donne's poetical gifts, Evelyn Simpson writes: "He was a poet who did not lose his poetical imagination when he entered the pulpit. Whenever he was deeply moved, his style caught fire, and he employed the images, the repetitions, and even sometimes the rhythms of poetry." Listen as John Donne tells of the death of the righteous in *Sermons,* VIII:

> They shall awake as Jacob did, and say as Jacob said, Surely the Lord is in this place, and this is no other but the house of God, and the gate of heasven, And into that gate they shall enter, and in that house they shall dwell, where there shall be no Cloud nor Sun, no darkenesse or dazling, but one equall light, no noyse nor silence, but one equal musick, no fears nor hopes, but one equall possession, no foes nor friends, but one equall communion and Identity, no ends nor beginnings, but one equall eternity. Keepe us Lord so awake in the duties of our Callings, that we may thus sleepe in thy peace, and wake in thy glory. . . .

The Sermons of John Donne contain some 160 sermons in all. In them one can enjoy the preacher's imaginative explications of biblical passages and his intense explorations of the themes of divine love and the decay and resurrection of the body.

John Donne was a consummate Christian thinker and preeminent poet of seventeenth-century England. He is among the greatest of Christian preachers. His sermons were publicly read long after his death and, together with his poems, have enjoyed a revival in the twentieth century. Modern poets have been much influenced by Donne's poetry. His prose is equal to his verse in beauty and power and is at its finest in the *Sermons.*

◆ Donne, John. *John Donne's Sermons on the Psalms and Gospels.* Evelyn M. Simpson, ed. Berkeley, Calif.: University of California Press, 1963.

◆ Potter, G. R., and E. M. Simpson. *The Sermons of John Donne.* Berkeley, Calif.: University of California Press, 1953–1962, 10 volumes.

. . . . *Holy Living* **1650**
Jeremy Taylor (1613–1667)

The English bishop and theological and devotional writer Jeremy Taylor was well-known as a preacher and as the author of some of the most noted religious works in English. He was born at Cambridge where he entered the university in 1626. There he was a student along with John Milton. Ordained in 1633, Taylor was a fellow of two Cambridge colleges, and chaplain to Archbishop Laud and to King Charles I. When the English Civil War broke out in 1642, Taylor left his rural church to serve with the royalist forces. The king's forces were defeated at Cardigan Castle in Wales, and he was briefly taken prisoner.

While England was under Puritan rule, Taylor remained in Wales to be chaplain to the second earl of Carbery. It was while living in Carbery's castle, Golden Grove, that Taylor wrote *Liberty of Prophesying* (1647), in which he argues for freedom of conscience and freedom of speech in a religious context. Next Taylor published *The Rule and Exercises of Holy Living* (1650). Holy living, he wrote, requires that people prepare for their heavenly destiny by limiting attractions to this world. Taylor rejected deathbed repentance, and so believed that these resolutions must be made before a person loses his or her strength.

In 1651 Taylor published *The Rule and Exercises of Holy Dying,* in which he declared that heaven is reserved for those who live and die in a holy manner—sober and godly in their earthly lives. Many readers, including Charles Wesley a century later, have found these books, usually cited simply as *Holy Living* and *Holy Dying,* of great spiritual benefit.

The following is a prayer to be recited when visiting the sick. It was written by Taylor and is found in the *Book of Common Prayer* (1928 American edition):

> O God, whose days are without end, and whose mercies cannot be numbered; Make us, we beseech thee, deeply sensible of the shortness and uncertainty of human life; and let thy Holy Spirit lead us in holiness and righteousness all our days: that, when we shall have served thee in our generation, we may be gathered unto our fathers, having the testimony of a good conscience; in the communion of the Catholic Church; in the confidence of a certain faith; in the comfort of a reasonable, religious, and holy hope; in favour with thee our God, and in perfect charity with the world. All which we ask through Jesus Christ our Lord.

The beauty of Taylor's writing caused him to be called the "Shakespeare of English divines," and "The Spenser of the pulpit." A number of his sermons are published, and many critics believe that Taylor's mastery of fine metaphor and his poetic imagination are best revealed in these sermons.

After the Restoration (1660), Taylor was made bishop of Down and Connor, in Ireland, and appointed vice-chancellor of Trinity College, Dublin. His term as bishop (1660–1667) was a period of turbulent dispute with the Presbyterian ministers who refused to acknowledge his jurisdiction over them. Perhaps they had not forgotten his broadside against them entitled *The Sacred Order and Offices of Episcopacy.* He had even less tolerance for Roman Catholics. This is seen in his somewhat violent *Dissuasive from Popery.*

At Dromore, Ireland, Taylor built the cathedral in which he is buried.

In *Holy Living* Taylor makes clear that religion is not confined merely to ritual worship: "As every man is wholly God's own portion by the title of creation: so all our labors and care, all our powers and faculties must be wholly employed in the service of God, even all the days of our life, that this life being ended, we may live with him for ever."

The book is structured according to Paul's statement in Titus 2:11-13 (KJV): "For the grace of God that bringeth salvation hath appeared to all men, Teaching us that, denying ungodliness and worldly lusts, we should live soberly, righteously, and godly, in this present world; Looking for that blessed hope, and the glorious appearing of the great God and our Savior Jesus Christ."

On the basis of this passage, Taylor divides Christian religious practice into three parts:

1. Sobriety—"all our deportment in our personal and private capacities, the fair treating of our bodies, and our spirits." This is the private practice of holy living—i.e., the duty toward oneself.
2. Justice—which "enlarges our duty in all relations to our neighbor." This is the public practice of holy living— i.e., the duty toward others.
3. Religion—which "contains the offices of direct religion and intercourse with God." This is the spiritual practice of holy living—i.e., the duty toward God.

The four chapters of the book first introduce the reader to the fundamental requirements of the life of religion and piety. The following three chapters each present one of the three aspects of Christian life.

Holy Living draws from three sources: the Bible, the church fathers, and the classics. Taylor was saturated with the language and ideas of the Bible and so frequently quotes it from memory, paraphrases it, and make free allusions to Scripture. Among the church fathers, he most frequently refers to Augustine and Jerome. But he also cites Gregory the Great, Bernard of Clairvaux, and others as authorities on moral or doctrinal issues and to clarify and amplify his arguments.

For Taylor, the classics were the writings of the philosophers Plutarch, Seneca, Aristotle, and Cicero; historians like Tacitus and Herodotus; poets such as Ovid, Horace, and Homer. These authors and many others like them are cited in conjunction with references to Scripture or the church fathers as sources of moral examples, authorities on ethical issues, and for decorative images.

Taylor described *Holy Living* as a "collection of holy precepts . . . rules for conduct of souls." He intended that it supply a need in "the want of personal and attending guides." So he wrote a comprehensive manual that extends to many if not all (in Taylor's understanding) areas and concerns of Christian life.

♦ Taylor, Jeremy. *Holy Living*. Edited by Hal M. Helms. Orleans, Mass.: Paraclete Press, 1988.

. . . . *Grace Abounding to the Chief of Sinners* 1666
John Bunyan (1628–1688)

John Bunyan was born at Elstow, Bedfordshire, the son of a traveling tinker, a mender of household utensils. He learned to read and write at a local school, and in 1644, during the English Civil War, he was pressed into military duty in the Parliamentarian army. Shortly after his discharge in 1647, Bunyan married and supported his family as a tinker. After reading two religious books that belonged to his wife, Bunyan experienced an awakened sense of religion and began to change many of his habits. Despite these outward changes, however, Bunyan realized a need for something deeper. One day he overheard a conversation about spiritual matters while pursuing his craft as a tinker. He was completely unfamiliar with the "inner experience" of which the people spoke, and this conversation eventually led to his conversion.

In 1653 Bunyan settled in Bedford and joined an independent congregation there. When he began preaching in 1657, news that the once-blaspheming tinker had turned preacher drew crowds from far away to hear him.

By 1656 Bunyan had published his first written work, a pamphlet against the Quakers called *Some Gospel Truths Opened.* This was answered by Edward Burroughs, an ardent Quaker, and Bunyan replied the following year with *A Vindication of Some Gospel Truths Opened.* His third work was a book about the parable of the rich man and Lazarus called *Sighs from Hell, or the Groans of a Damned Soul* (1658).

In 1660 persecution against Nonconformists (those who did not conform to the practices of the Church of England) was revived. Meeting houses were closed; all persons were required to attend their parish church; and it was illegal to conduct worship services except in accordance with Anglican ritual. Bunyan continued to preach in barns, in private homes, under trees, or in churches if invited. He was arrested in November 1660 on his way to conduct a religious service.

While in prison Bunyan received unrestricted visitors and continued to write and publish. At this time he wrote *Grace Abounding to the Chief of Sinners, Christian Behavior,* and *The Holy City.* In the early days of his imprisonment, he attended Bedford Church, but after October 1661 his name was not again on the attendance record until October 1668; evidently his confinement became stricter. After 1668 he appears to have been paroled, although his formal pardon did not come until 1672.

Bunyan published his famous allegory, *The Pilgrim's Progress,* in 1678. Early in the Christian tradition, pilgrimage had come to represent the journey through life or the progress of human life to a state of blessedness. In *The Pilgrim's Progress* the pilgrim is a human soul in quest of peace with God.

The Pilgrim's Progress was followed by two more allegorical books, *The Life and Death of Mr. Badman* (1680) and *The Holy War* (1682). In 1684 Bunyan published a *Second Part to the Pilgrim's Progress,* a sequel in which Pilgrim's wife and children, accompanied by Mercy, follow the same route traced in the first book and enter the Celestial City.

Both *The Pilgrim's Progress* and its sequel draw from Bunyan's earlier work, *Grace Abounding to the Chief of Sinners.* This is an introspective autobiographical sketch of his conversion, call to ministry, and imprisonment.

Grace Abounding belongs to the genre of Puritan writing called *spiritual autobiography.* In such works an author tells of God's grace, working to accomplish conversion, and often concludes with an account of the author's persecution by civil authorities and imprisonment for conscience's sake. Bunyan's *Grace Abounding* is outstanding among the works of this genre. As is typical, it concentrates on the inner working of grace rather than events in chronology. But the author's ability to express his spiritual conflicts in thoughtful and dramatic prose sets this book above similar writing.

For example, after telling of a rebuke he received from a woman for his swearing and cursing, Bunyan writes:

> While I stood there, and hanging down my head, I wished with all my heart that I might be a little child again, that my father might learn me to speak without this wicked way of swearing: for, thought I, I am so accustomed to it, that it is but in vain for me to think of a reformation, for I thought it could never be.

But how it came to pass I know not, I did from this time forward so leave my swearing, that it was a great wonder to my self to observe it; and whereas before I knew not how to speak unless I put an oath before, and another behind, to make my words have authority, now, I could, without it, speak better, and with more pleasantness than ever I could before: all this while I knew not Jesus Christ, neither did I leave my sports and play. When Bunyan wrote the classic religious allegory, *The Pilgrim's Progress*, he transferred his personal experience into figurative terms. So *Grace Abounding* is a vital introduction to *The Pilgrim's Progress*. In fact it may be a more accessible work to readers today, for the modern believer may more readily identify and recognize the experiences of John Bunyan rather than the allegorical Pilgrim. An example of such personal reflection in *Grace Abounding* can be seen in Bunyan's remembrance of the words of Luke 14:22-23: "Compel them to come in, that my house may be filled, and yet there is room." These were "sweet words to me; for truly, I thought that by them I saw there was place enough in Heaven for me, and, moreover, that when the Lord Jesus did speak these words, he then did think of me."

◆ Bunyan, John. *Grace Abounding to the Chief of Sinners.* Edited by W. R. Owens. New York: Viking Penguin, 1987.

. . . . *Christian Perfection*
François Fénelon (1651–1715)

François Fénelon was born in southern France, educated at the seminary of St. Sulpice in Paris, and ordained to the priesthood in 1675. From 1678 to 1689 Fénelon supervised the Catholiques Nouvelles, a house for Protestant converts. During this time he wrote his *Traite de l'Education des Filles (An Essay on the Education of Girls),* published in 1687, in which he insists that education begin at an early age and on the instruction of girls in all the duties of their future in life. The religious teaching he recommends is solid enough to enable them to refute heresies if necessary. He also advises a more serious course of studies than was then customary.

Between 1689 and 1697 he acted as tutor to King Louis XIV's grandson, the duke of Burgundy, for whom he wrote his educational novel *Les Aventures de Telemaque*, completed and posthumously published in 1717. In this book, under the guise of pleasant fiction, he taught the young prince lessons of self-control and all the duties required by his exalted position. Telemaque's implied criticism of the misrule of Louis XIV is said to have angered the king, but many feel that if the Duke of Burgundy had lived to be king, Fénelon would have been prime minister of France.

In 1688 Fénelon became acquainted with Madame Jeanne Marie Guyon, whose Quietist practices he at first approved and defended. In 1696, however, he signed the thirty-four articles of Issy, which condemned Quietism. In 1697 he published his *Explications des Maximes des Saints,* a series of articles on mysticism. Each article was divided into two paragraphs, one laying down the true, the other the false, teaching concerning the love of God. In this work he undertook to distinguish clearly every step in the upward way of the spiritual life. The final end of the Christian soul is pure love of God, without any admixture of self-interest, a love in which neither fear of punishment nor desire of reward has any part. This book was condemned by the pope in 1699, who accused Fénelon of "having loved God too much, and man too little." Fénelon was subsequently banished from the French royal palace at Versailles.

Appointed archbishop of Cambrai in 1695, Fénelon won a reputation in his diocese as a diligent and benevolent, though autocratic, administrator as well as an effective and influential preacher. During the Flemish wars, Fénelon turned his palace into a hospital, cared for impoverished peasants, and fed the French army.

Christian Perfection is a collection of writings of François Fénelon—primarily his letters—and from conferences he held at the shamelessly immoral court of Louis XIV. Here is a sample of Fénelon's counsel:

> Our time for social contacts and diversion is the most dangerous for us, and can be the most useful for others. At that time we must be on guard, that is, more faithful in the presence of God. The practice of Christian vigilance so recommended by our Lord, the aspiration and elevation of mind and heart toward God, not only as a habit but actually doing so much as possible in the simple light of faith, the gentle and peaceful dependence of the soul upon grace, which it recognizes as the only basis of its safety and of its strength; all this ought to be called upon to keep the soul from the subtle poison which is often hidden in conversation and recreation, and to let it know how to use wisely an opportunity to teach and influence others. This is especially necessary for those in positions of great power, and for those whose words can do great good or great harm.

The 1947 Harper & Row edition, edited by Charles F. Whiston, is arranged in two sections with similar subjects placed together. Whiston writes: "Part I deals with the very practical task of seeking to live the life of Christian perfection in the world. It is largely composed of letters written to people living at court and in the world. Part II deals in a more extended and complete way with important aspects of the Christian life."

Whiston makes the following observation about Fénelon's view of the Christian life as seen in *Christian Perfection:*

> In reading these letters we shall be helped if we keep in mind constantly a note, central in Fénelon's whole life and teaching, but which is often not a central note in our religious thinking and living today. It is the great Christian notion of *theocentricity,* that in all true and Christian religion God

Himself is the main and central factor. We today are so apt to think of religion from a human centered perspective, and thus think of religion as our acts and words and life toward God and man. But Fénelon's perspective is not ours. For him, religion is primarily that which God himself wills and does in and upon man. It is He who is utterly sovereign in history even over the slightest details. . . . Man's central act is to abandon his life into the hands of God's wise and loving sovereignty, and one by one to stop every inner resistance to God's redemptive work in him.

One may think that a spiritual book originating with the seventeenth-century French aristocracy would perceive of the Christian life in grim terms. But Fénelon says, "Christian perfection is not so severe, tiresome, and constraining as we think. It asks us to be God's from the bottom of our hearts. And since we thus are God's, everything that we do for him is easy."

◆ Fénelon, François. *Christian Perfection.* Edited by Charles F. Whiston. New York: Harper & Row, 1947.

◆ Fénelon, François. *Christian Perfection.* Minneapolis: Bethany House, 1996.

. . . . *Pensées* **1670**
Blaise Pascal (1623–1662)

The French mathematician, theologian, physicist, and man-of-letters Blaise Pascal was born at Clermont-Ferrand, France. He was the son of the local president of the court of exchequer (who managed the royal revenue). Pascal's mother died in 1630, and the family moved to Paris, where his father personally undertook his children's education. But the young Pascal was not allowed to begin a subject until his father thought he could easily master it.

As a result, when the time came for mathematics it was discovered that the eleven-year-old boy had already worked out the first twenty-three of Euclid's theorems.

At sixteen Pascal published a paper on solid geometry that Descartes refused to believe was the handiwork of a youth. In 1647 Pascal patented a calculating machine he had built to simplify his father's accounting tasks. The machine was based on a system of rotating disks—the foundation of arithmetical machines until modern times. Pascal also invented the barometer and the syringe and first described the principles of hydraulics. Pascal's papers on the area of the cycloid (1661) preceded the invention of differential calculus.

In 1646 the entire Pascal family was converted to Jansenism, a reform movement in Roman Catholicism. Pascal's sister, Jacqueline, entered the Jansenist convent at Port-Royal, but Pascal divided his time between mathematics and the Parisian social scene. Then on November 23, 1654, Pascal heard a sermon at Port-Royal that brought about a profound religious experience. That night he had the first of two mystical visions. He described his experience on a piece of parchment, which he sewed into the lining of his coat. The parchment was found at his death. It said, "Fire. God of Abraham, God of Isaac, God of Jacob, not of the philosophers and scholars. Certainty, certainty, heartfelt joy, peace. God of Jesus Christ. Joy, joy, joy, oceans of joy!"

Pascal joined his sister at her retreat at Port-Royal, withdrew from mathematics and social life, and joined the battle of the Jansenists against the Jesuits of the Sorbonne, who had publicly denounced Arnauld, the Jansenist mathematician, as a heretic.

Pascal wrote eighteen brilliant pamphlets, published as the *Provincial Letters* (1656–1657). He attacked, in superb language, the Jesuits' meaningless jargon, fallacious reasoning, and moral laxity and supported the Jansenists' demand for a reemphasis on Augustine's doctrine of grace within the Catholic church. One hundred years later the heretical Voltaire was extravagant in his praise of Pascal's moderate and pious prose masterpiece of the French language. "The first work of genius that appeared in prose was *The Provincial Letters,*" wrote Voltaire. "Examples of every species of eloquence may there be found. There is not a single word in it that, after one hundred years, has undergone the change to which all living languages are liable. We may identify this work with the era when our language became fixed." Though *The Provincial Letters* failed to save Arnauld, it powerfully undermined Jesuit authority and prestige.

In 1658 Pascal began an *Apology for the Christian Religion,* but at age thirty-nine Pascal died before completing the work. Fragments of this work were discovered after his death. These remarkable notes were published as *Pensées (Thoughts)* in 1670. This work, a classic of literature and apologetics, contains profound insight into religious truths coupled with skepticism of rational thought and theology. In part it pits the case for vital Christianity against the rationalism of Descartes and the skepticism of the French writer Montaigne.

In *Pensées,* Pascal noted that man's need for God is made evident by his misery apart from God, his constant need for diversion, and his resort to the world of the imagination. God can be known through an act of faith, itself given by God. Pascal held that the supporting evidence for the truth of Christianity is overwhelming, including fulfilled prophecies, miracles, the witness of history, and the self-authentication of Scripture. Even beyond these strong external evidences, however, God is known by the heart. "The heart," wrote Pascal, "has its reasons which the reason does not know."

In all of Pascal's writing, both religious and scientific, there is a total absence of obscure and technical jargon. He was neither a specialist nor a professional in any of his activities. He was a restless pursuer of truth:

> Let man contemplate Nature in its entirety, high and majestic; let him expand his gaze from the lowly objects which surround him. Let him look on this blazing light, placed like an eternal lamp in order to light up the universe; let him see that this earth is but a point compared to the vast circle which this star describes and let him marvel at the fact that this vast orbit itself is merely a tiny point compared to the stars which roll through the firmament.

In mathematics, physics, and faith Pascal's method was the same: Find a hypothesis and test it against every aspect of the problem. If it survives this testing, the hypothesis is accepted. Pascal investigated and confirmed various concepts in this way, including thoughts about the hexagram, barometric pressure, original sin, incarnation, and redemption.

Pensées is valued by all sorts of people—religious, aesthetic, and philosophical—as a sort of gospel. Pascal's thoughts trace the universal search for God. He cuts across doctrine into the heart of the moral problem. With passion for truth and spiritual honesty, he appeals to the intellect. With lucid expression, genuine sentiment, and an almost merciless description of humanity without God, he appeals to the heart. Pascal's *Pensées* is a clear, living explanation of the Christian faith.

♦ Pascsal, Blaise. *Pensées* (Penguin Classics). Translated by A. J. Krailsheimer. New York: Penguin, 1995.

················ *The Practice of the Presence of God* c. **1693**
Brother Lawrence (1611–1691)

Nicholas Herman (later known as Brother Lawrence) was born in Lorraine, France. After an obscure and apparently poor childhood, Herman had an experience of conversion at the age of eighteen and entered the French army during the Thirty Years' War. He was a soldier for eighteen years. Later, in Paris, he served as a servant to the treasurer of France. While there, Herman was attracted to the severe order of Discalced Carmelite Brothers. Around 1651 he made his profession in this order, took the name Brother Lawrence, and continued there for the remainder of his life. He never advanced (nor seems to have desired to advance) beyond the status of lay brother, served the community in its kitchen for thirty years, was released from his duties because of blindness, and died a few years later.

Brother Lawrence left no major writings except for a few spiritual notes, letters, and a short manuscript entitled *Maxims.* Collected by his abbot, Joseph de Beaufort, these were later found in Beaufort's room along with added accounts of conversations the abbot had had with Lawrence. The simple writings were assembled and published in 1691. Two years later a shorter version was published, some of which has been translated, edited, and published as *The Practice of the Presence of God.*

This book is a collection of Lawrence's reflections on everything from prayer to daily work. In his letters Lawrence reveals his desire for deep intimacy with God. The personal interviews with Brother Lawrence discuss his way to become established in God's presence. This is done, says Lawrence, "by continually conversing with Him. [It is] a shameful thing to quit His conversation to think of trifles and fooleries." At the time of these conversations, Lawrence had been working in the monastery kitchen for fifteen years. He had found God present in every situation of his life. His writings encourage believers to attempt to perform every action with this understanding.

In reading *The Practice of the Presence of God,* one can see that Brother Lawrence tried to conduct his life by the love of God, performing every deed by this single motivation. Lawrence was not impressed with good works. He was concerned that good works reveal the love of God in the heart of the one performing them.

Lawrence proclaimed, "To be with God there is no need to be continually in church. Of our heart we may make an oratory, wherein to retire from time to time and with Him hold meek, humble loving converse." For Brother Lawrence, God could be encountered anywhere, although it is important to understand that Lawrence was not denying the need for believers to attend church. He was simply trying to remove the barriers between sacred and secular life. Lawrence insisted that "the time of action is not different from that of prayer. I enjoy God with as great tranquillity in the hurry of my kitchen, where frequently many people call upon me at the same time for different things, as if I was on my knees at the holy sacrament."

◆ Brother Lawrence. *The Practice of the Presence of God.* Edited by Hal H. Helms. Orleans, Mass.: Paraclete, 1996.

The Eighteenth
and Nineteenth
Centuries

William Law (1686–1761)

William Law was born at King's Cliffe, Northampton-
shire, England, to a family of substantial means. He attended
Emmanuel College, Cambridge, where he became a fellow.
In 1712, a year after his ordination, he earned a master of arts
degree, following intensive study in the classics and philosophy. It was probably at this time that he began to read the early
English mystics and became acquainted with classical devotional writers, such as St. Francis de Sales and Thomas à
Kempis.

When the Hanoverian king George I came to the throne,
Law refused to take an oath of allegiance. As a result he lost
his fellowship at the university and permanently lost the right
to preach in the Church of England.

Little is known of Law's actions after this, but it is believed
that he went to London. In 1723 Law became affiliated with the
Gibbon family in Putney, where he served as tutor and chaplain
to the household. After Edward Gibbon died, the household

broke up in 1737, and Law returned to his native King's Cliffe, where he remained for the rest of his life. In his later years, Law, together with Sarah Hutchinson and Hester Gibbon, founded several almshouses and a school.

Law wrote a number of works. His first significant writing was *Three Letters to the Bishop of Bangor* (1717), an effective apologetic for orthodox Christianity. In his *Practical Treatise Upon Christian Perfection* (1726), he laid down rules for achieving a life of piety. Law's most notable work, however, is *A Serious Call to a Devout and Holy Life* (1728). Though Law's writing lacks an emphasis upon Christ's redemptive ministry, its insight into devotional life influenced such evangelists as George Whitefield and John Wesley.

William Law wrote *A Serious Call* while still in his early thirties. In it he raised a formidable challenge to the unbelieving age in which he lived and profoundly influenced many minds of his time. Samuel Johnson commented on his encounter with *A Serious Call to a Devout and Holy Life* while a student at Oxford. He said, "I expected to find it a dull book . . . but I found Law quite an overmatch for me." Law presented his arguments in a way that made it credible to believe in Christianity without losing intellectual integrity.

The basic premise throughout *A Serious Call* assumes that the devout person is centered in God. Law said that a devout life is "a better sacrifice to God than any forms of holy and heavenly prayers." Law believed that devotion to God is humanity's highest attainment and that true freedom is expressed in the believer's devotion to the Redeemer-God. This devotion is a sign of true genius, "a soul in its highest state of knowledge."

The first half of the book sets a standard for honoring God in outward affairs. The second half is a guide to prayer and the ordering of the inner life. Law gives specific instructions for prayer and for the right use of money. According to Law, every area of life should reflect the believer's devotion to God.

◆ Law, William. *A Serious Call to a Devout and Holy Life.* The Classics of Western Spirituality series. New York: Paulist, 1978.

. . . . *A Treatise Concerning Religious Affections* **1746**
Jonathan Edwards (1703–1758)

Jonathan Edwards was born in East Windsor, Connecticut. There he received his early education from his father, a Congregational minister. He entered Yale College at the age of thirteen, graduated in 1720, and remained at the college until August 1722 to study for the ministry. After a brief stint as the minister of a Scottish Presbyterian church in New York, Edwards returned to Yale in 1723. There he passed the examination for a master of arts degree and became a tutor at the college in 1724.

Edwards's grandfather, Solomon Stoddard, was the minister at Northampton, Massachusetts. Jonathan Edwards became the aging pastor's assistant in 1726. Stoddard died in 1729, and Edwards assumed his ministry. He quickly established a reputation as a preacher and advocate of experiential religion. Under Edwards's influence Northampton and neighboring parishes entered a powerful spiritual awakening in 1734–1735. Again in 1739 Edwards induced a religious revival. This one extended further afield and has come to be known as the Great Awakening.

At this time Edwards met the English revivalist George Whitefield, who spread the American's fame abroad. The most famous sermon in American history was preached by Edwards during the Awakening in Enfield, Connecticut. This is titled "Sinners in the Hands of an Angry God" (1741).

In Northampton, Edwards wanted to restrict access to Communion to only those who could give proper proof of their conversion. The resultant controversy caused his dismissal by the church in Northampton. The following year (1751) he became pastor of the church in Stockbridge, Massachusetts, and served as teacher and missionary to the nearby Housatonic Indians.

Then, in 1758 Jonathan Edwards accepted the presidency of the College of New Jersey (later Princeton University), but within a month of assuming these duties, he died from the effects of a smallpox inoculation.

Edwards was both a practical and theoretical theologian. He is widely considered the most important theologian of his day and one of the greatest thinkers America has produced. His approach to the Christian faith is based on two strong points. First, Edwards insisted that sin was elemental opposition to God and that salvation meant a radical change of heart. Such change is dependent upon the absolute sovereignty of God. Second, he taught that salvation is not simply a rational understanding of God or biblical truth. Rather it is a supernatural work of God in the heart of the believer. America's greatest theologian taught that true religion is a matter of the heart, not the mind.

Among his many writings, Edwards's most mature analysis of religious experience is *A Treatise Concerning Religious Affections* (1746). In it Edwards insists the essence of all true religion lies in holy love. Herein is its great value as devotional literature.

During the Great Awakening, Edwards saw that people had many powerful inward experiences of God. But outward expressions of grace in people's lives were rare. In *Religious Affections* Edwards tried to develop a reliable series of signs by which genuine religious affections (his term for the expressions of God's grace) could be distinguished from other, perhaps counterfeit, feelings. Edwards had lost confidence in subjective forms of religious consciousness. He had learned that these could be forms of self-deception. Instead, he relied on publicly manifested Christian practice as the true test of religious experience.

The book is divided into three parts. The first defines the nature of religious experience, noting that true religion is primarily a matter of the heart and is seated in the affections. The second identifies and examines false signs of true religion. The third, which takes up nearly three quarters of the treatise, describes twelve marks that arise from a genuine religious conversion.

The author uses 1 Peter 1:8 as the starting point for his compelling argument: "Whom having not seen, ye love; in whom, though now ye see him not, yet believing, ye rejoice with joy unspeakable and full of glory" (KJV). From this verse Edwards develops his view of true religion: It consists of the affections of love and joy in Christ. Love depends on the spiritual sight of faith, while joy is the fruit of that faith. From this text he eventually derives the doctrine: "True religion, in great part, consists of only affections." Such affections are exercises of the believer's will. They seek to possess divine glory in pure love. To Edwards, pure love is both the source of all true religious affections and the chief affection itself.

The third and most substantial section of *Religious Affections* gives an exhaustive account of twelve signs of religious affections. Edwards emphasizes that these signs are not for discerning true or false affections in others, but rather they should be used to examine one's own self.

As Edwards discusses the first sign, he fleshes out the biblical meanings of *spiritual, supernatural,* and *divine.* These are the only influences that produce genuine affections. The second sign is that a person's love for God is not dependent on the belief that God loves him or has forgiven him. Third, if an affection springs from an individual's concern for his own welfare, it is false. Fourth, gracious affections are based on spiritual understanding; therefore, they involve the will and the heart rather than mental speculation or observation.

The fifth sign shows that genuine affections are accompanied by an immediate certainty of the truth of religion. Sixth, true affection involves voluntary humiliation before God. Seventh, true affections include a change of nature that, although not instantaneous or complete, is known by its permanence.

Signs eight and nine indicate that the believer should face the world with meekness and tenderness. The tenth sign evaluates the symmetry of God's workmanship in a believer, emphasizing balance in the believer's life. The eleventh sign is an increase in the believer's appetite for God rather than an increase in self-satisfaction.

Sign twelve is to Edwards "the chief of all the signs of grace." That is, holy affections are seen in the believer's daily practice. Jonathan Edwards said, "Men's deeds are better and more faithful interpreters of their minds than their words." In other words, A repentant believer's actions speak louder than words.

◆ Edwards, Jonathan. *Religious Affections: A Christian's Character before God.* Classics of Faith and Devotion. Edited by James M. Houston. Eugene, Oreg.: Bethany House, 1996.

. . . . *Diary of David Brainerd* **1749**
David Brainerd (1718–1747)

The diary of David Brainerd, though not written for publication, influenced hundreds to pursue a life of prayer and communion with God and moved scores to give their lives to Christian missionary work.

David Brainerd was born at Haddam, Connecticut, the sixth child and third son in the family of Connecticut legislator Hezekiah Brainerd. Though his father died when David was nine years old, and his mother passed away when he was fourteen, Brainerd's early years were spent in an atmosphere of piety divided between farming, reading the Bible, and praying. He was converted in 1739. Here are his remarks about that event:

> As I was walking in a dark thick grove, "unspeakable glory" seemed to open to the view and apprehension of my soul. . . . It was a new inward apprehension or view that I had of God; such as I never had before, nor anything that I had the least remembrance of. So that I stood still and wondered and admired. . . . I had now no particular apprehension of any one person of the Trinity, either the Father, Son, or Holy Spirit, but it appeared to be divine glory and splendor that I then beheld. And my soul "rejoiced with joy unspeakable" to see such a God, such a glorious divine being, and I was inwardly pleased and satisfied that he should be God over all forever and ever. My soul was so captivated and delighted with the excellency, the loveliness, and the greatness and other perfections of God that I was even swallowed up in him, at least to that degree that I had no thought, as I remember at first, about my own salvation or scarce that there was such a creature as I.
>
> Thus the Lord, I trust, brought me to a hearty desire to exalt him, to set him on the throne and to "seek first his Kingdom," i.e., principally and ultimately to aim at his honor and glory as the King and sovereign of the universe, which is the foundation of the religion of Jesus.

Later that year Brainerd entered Yale College to prepare for the ministry. At this time tensions had developed within the school—the students were more spiritually aware than the less-excited faculty and staff. Brainerd was overheard to say that tutor Chauncey Whittelsey "has no more grace than a chair" and that he wondered why the Rector "did not drop down dead" for fining students for their evangelical zeal. He also attended a revival meeting forbidden by the rector. So, even though he stood first in his class, Brainerd was expelled from Yale in 1742 without graduating. He completed his studies privately until he was licensed to preach by the Association of Ministers in Fairfield County, Connecticut.

But by Connecticut law, no one who had not graduated from Harvard, Yale, or a European university could be established as a minister. So it was that Brainerd was appointed missionary to the Indians under the auspices of the Society in Scotland for the Propagation of Christian Knowledge, founded in 1709. He began his work with the Housatonic Indians at Kaunaumeek about twenty miles northwest of Stockbridge, Massachusetts. Jonathan Edwards wrote of this beginning:

> And, having put his hand to the plow, he looked not
> back, and gave himself, heart, soul, and mind, and strength,
> to his chosen mission with unfaltering purpose, with
> apostolic zeal, with a heroic faith that feared no danger
> and surmounted every obstacle, and with an earnestness
> of mind that wrought wonders on savage lives and whole
> communities.

Next Brainerd preached to the Indians at the forks of the Delaware River in Pennsylvania for one year. Then in June 1744, he was ordained by the Presbytery at Newark, New Jersey. In June 1745, he first went to the Native Americans at Crossweeksung (now Crosswicks), New Jersey. There, unable to speak the native language, Brainerd worked mainly by prayer. He asked that the power of the Holy Spirit would come upon him so that his hearers would not be able to refuse the gospel message. This evidently occurred. He once preached through an interpreter who was so intoxicated that he could hardly stand up. Scores were converted through that sermon. Within a year there were 130 persons in a growing assembly of believers.

After two years of labor in New Jersey, plagued by ill health and the hardships of the primitive conditions, Brainerd retired to the home of Jonathan Edwards in Northampton, Massachusetts, in May 1747. There he died of tuberculosis.

Soon after Brainerd's death, Edwards published an account of Brainerd's life and his diary (1749). David Brainerd's story is not upbeat or dynamic. His life was one of constant struggle with sickness, depression, loneliness, and physical hardship. He was kicked out of college and died young. His work had hardly begun when it was over. Yet many, many people have been profoundly affected by this man's diary.

John Wesley said, "Let every preacher read carefully over the *Life of David Brainerd.*" Henry Martyn, missionary to the Jews, read the book and was "filled with a holy emulation of that extraordinary man; and after deep consideration and fervent prayer, he was at length fixed in a resolution to imitate his example." William Carey, the famous missionary to China, called Edwards's *Life of David Brainerd* a sacred text. The book exerted a deep influence in promoting the cause of Christian missions. It is cited by Robert M'Cheyne of Scotland, David Livingstone of England, Andrew Murray of South Africa, and Jim Elliot of the United States.

Brainerd tells of sickness: "Rode several hours in the rain through the howling wilderness, although I was so disordered in body that little or nothing but blood came from me." He decries his depression: "Was so overwhelmed with dejection that I knew not how to live: I longed for death exceedingly: My soul was 'sunk in deep waters,' and 'the floods' were ready to 'drown me': I was so much oppressed that my soul was in a kind of horror." His loneliness is difficult to imagine: "Most of the talk I hear is either Highland Scotch or Indian. I have no fellow Christian to whom I might unbosom myself and lay open my spiritual sorrows, and with whom I might take sweet counsel in conversation about heavenly things, and join in social prayer." His physical discomfort is equally difficult to imagine: "I live poorly with regard to the comforts of life: most of my diet consists of boiled corn, hasty pudding, etc. I lodge on a bundle of straw, and my labor is hard and extremely difficult; and I have little experience of success to comfort me." But his love is warmly evident: "Felt my heat drawn out after God in prayer, almost all the forenoon; especially while riding. And in the evening, could not help crying to God for those poor Indians; and after I went to bed my heart continued to go out to God for them, till I dropped asleep. Oh, 'Blessed be God that I may pray!'" Though he was sometimes cool: "About noon, rode up to the Indians; and while going, could feel no desires for them, and even dreaded to say anything to 'em."

Brainerd's is a story of disappointment, of frustration. But it has inspired so many because, perhaps unknowingly, David Brainerd lived according to this basic principal of the gospel: "Except a corn of wheat fall into the ground and die, it abideth alone: but if it die, it bringeth forth much fruit" (John 12:24, KJV).

♦ Brainerd, David. *Memoirs of the Reverend David Brainerd: Missionary to the Indians on the Border of New York, New Jersey & Pennsylvania.* St. Clair Shores, Mich.: Scholarly Press, 1970.

♦ Edwards, Jonathan. *Life of David Brainerd.* (The Works of Jonathan Edwards). New Haven, Conn.: Yale University Press, 1985.

♦ Howard, Philip E., and Jonathan Edwards. *The Life and Diary of David Brainerd.* Grand Rapids: Baker Book House, 1989.

♦ On-line at the Christian Classics Ethereal Library at Calvin College http://www.ccel.org.

........*Journal* **1771**

John Woolman (1720–1772)

Born in Northampton, New Jersey, John Woolman was the
son of a farmer. His Quaker grandfather had been among the first
settlers in west New Jersey, just across the Delaware River from
Pennsylvania, the center of Quaker settlement in America. As a
young man, John Woolman moved to Mount Holly, where he
worked as a tailor. He owned a tailor shop for a time, and this
trade supported him at various times throughout his life. But
Woolman desired a deeper spirituality, and this led him to simplify
his life. He became a recorded minister of the Society of Friends
(1743) and for thirty-seven years served as chairman for the quar-
terly business meeting in Burlington County. He then began to
travel extensively, ministering to Quaker communities throughout
the colonies, making thirty-nine such trips in twenty-five years.
Woolman died of smallpox on a visit to England in 1772.

John Woolman's *Journal* reveals a man who desired to follow
the "pure leading" of God, undistorted by natural human self-
interest. His first entry says, in part, "I have often felt a motion
of love to leave some hints in writing of my experience of the
goodness of God." He was conspicuous, even among Quakers,
for his intense mystical piety. The *Journal* shows how deeply
God's goodness was integrated into his living. He wrote:

> It was my concern from day to day to say neither more nor
> less than what the spirit of truth opened in me, being jeal-
> ous over myself lest I should say anything to make my
> testimony look agreeable to that mind in people which is
> not in pure obedience to the cross of Christ.

Woolman's America was a world of economic growth and
agricultural expansion. The need for labor brought African
slaves. The need for land resulted in war with the Indians. Into

this world of slavery, Indian abuse, and war, Woolman desired to bring reform. He was concerned that Friends not take part in the injustices that seemed to pervade colonial America. He believed that most, if not all, of society's problems could be traced to the pervasive principle of selfish pragmatism. In remedy, he called his fellow Quakers to live according to the principle of selfless love.

Woolman preached and wrote against slavery during a time when the practice was little questioned. His testimony caused Quakers at the Philadelphia yearly meeting to denounce slavery in 1776. As a result of his efforts, many Friends, even some in the southern colonies, chose to free their slaves. Woolman also preached and wrote against the abuse of Indians, the ill-treatment of the poor, and conscription and taxation to support the war effort.

He was a prophetic voice to colonial America, but his influence was felt only significantly among the small population of Friends. Yet a century after his death, his writings (*Some Considerations on the Keeping of Negroes* and his *Journal*) made notable impact upon the abolitionist movement in the nineteenth century. Woolman's call to deeper spiritual life, defense of the helpless, and selfless action speaks to Christians of all centuries.

The *Journal* has become a classic among Quaker works. He began writing it when he was thirty-six years old and continued it until his death. In 1871 the poet John Greenleaf Whittier published the *Journal* with an informative introduction. This edition went through a number of printings, and Woolman's *Journal* was eventually chosen for inclusion among the Harvard Classics. These are the beginning sentences of Whittier's introduction:

> To those who judge by the outward appearance, nothing is more difficult of explanation than the strength of moral influence often exerted by obscure and uneventful lives. Some

great reform which lifts the world to a higher level, some mighty change for which the ages have waited in anxious expectancy, takes place before our eyes, and, in seeking to trace it back to its origin, we are often surprised to find the initial link in the chain of causes to be some comparatively obscure individual, the divine commission and significance of whose life were scarcely understood by his contemporaries, and perhaps not even by himself.

John Woolman's *Journal* records his spiritual development as he worked and traveled among the Society of Friends in colonial America. In it he notes the development of his sensitive conscience that compelled him to publicly express his convictions. His *Journal* is a story of religious growth, which, for Woolman, began before he was seven years old.

From animals to Indians to slaves, Woolman repeatedly expressed his concern for those who were abused and considered of little significance. Because Woolman was literate, unlike most Americans of his day, he was often called upon to draw up legal documents. Once when he was compelled to write the bill of sale for a slave, Woolman became so uneasy in his conscience that he denounced slavery even as he wrote the bill. Shortly afterward he began his lifelong crusade against slavery.

Woolman is given credit for the abolition of slavery among the Society of Friends before the Revolution. But it did not stop there. As Whittier wrote in his introduction to the *Journal*: "A far-reaching moral, social, and political revolution, undoing the evil work of centuries, unquestionably owes much of its original impulse to the life and labors of a poor, unlearned workingman of New Jersey, whose very existence was scarcely known beyond the narrow circle of his religious society."

Woolman's *Journal* also records how he refused to use many things because of the connection with slavery. For example, he refused to eat sugar or wear dyed cloth. When crossing to England, Woolman's conscience would not allow him even to take space in the cabin of the ship. The *Journal* is a glimpse into a heart of deep conviction and piety. Although in many ways eccentric even among Quakers, Whittier observes:

> It will be noted throughout the *Journal* . . . that in his life-long testimony against wrong he never lost sight of the oneness of humanity, its common responsibility, its fellowship of suffering and communion of sin. Few have ever had so profound a conviction of the truth of the Apostle's declaration that no man liveth and no man dieth to himself.

♦ Woolman, John. *The Journal and Major Essays of John Woolman.* Edited by Phillips P. Moulton. New York: Oxford University Press, 1971; Richmond, Ind.: Friends United Press, 1989.

♦ Quotes from Whittier taken from *The Journal of John Woolman.* Boston: James R. Osgood and Company, 1871.

. . . . *Journal* c. 1791
John Wesley (1703–1791)

Born in Epworth, England, in 1703, John Wesley was the fifteenth child and second surviving son of Susanna and Samuel Wesley. Samuel was a former Nonconformist and rector at Epworth. He and his wife raised their children in an atmosphere of piety and Puritan discipline. John was educated at the Charterhouse School, London, and Christ Church, Oxford. He was elected fellow of Lincoln College, Oxford, in 1726, and received the master of arts in 1727. Wesley's short tenure as assistant to his father at Wroote (1727–1729) was his only experience in a parish.

A letter from the rector of Lincoln brought Wesley back to his duties at Oxford, where he joined his brother Charles, George

Whitefield, and others in a venture that was to be the cradle of the Methodist movement. These earnest young men caused a sensation at Oxford by frequently meeting together for Bible study, Communion, and prayer. They were derisively referred to as the "Holy Club," "Sacramentarians," "Bible moths" (feeding on the Bible as moths on cloth), "Bible bigots," and "Methodists." John was called the "curator" or "father" of the Holy Club. Charles had started the group while John was away serving at Wroote. Charles said that they were given the name *Methodist* because of their strict conformity to the method of biblical study prescribed by the university. John would later redefine this term in his *English Dictionary* as "one that lives according to the *method* laid down in the Bible. The Methodist controversy eventually cost Wesley the loss of earnings, friends, and reputation, but he still insisted that it was worth it in order to gain a pure heart.

That same year the Holy Club began to dissolve when John, Charles, and two others of its members sailed for the American colony of Georgia. John was to serve as missionary to the native Americans and pastor of the Savannah parish, but a failed romance with Sophia Hopkey, niece of the chief magistrate of Savannah, contributed to the failure of this endeavor. In addition, although Wesley had faithfully served his flock, he exhibited a high churchmanship that antagonized the parish. Eventually Wesley left Georgia and returned to England.

Although Wesley's ministry in America was less than successful, an experience on his voyage to Georgia dramatically impacted his later work. During a violent storm, Wesley was cowering in fear of death, but he noticed a group of Moravian Brethren who were remarkably calm. An interview with the Moravians' leader upon landing in Georgia set in motion Wesley's search for the living reality of the doctrines he preached.

On January 24, 1738, shortly after his return from Georgia, Wesley wrote in his *Journal:* "I went to America to convert the Indians; but O! who shall convert me? Who, what is he that shall deliver me from this evil heart of unbelief? . . . O who will deliver me from this fear of death?"

Back in London John met Peter Bohler, a Moravian, who instructed him that salvation comes by faith. Wesley also read Luther's commentary on Galatians, which emphasizes justification by faith alone. Then Wesley attended a Moravian meeting in May of 1738, near his old school, Charterhouse. There he experienced what he described as a strange warming of his heart. He came to believe that he was indeed forgiven of his sin and had received salvation from the law of sin and death.

Eighteen days after Wesley's experience at Charterhouse, John preached at Oxford University his famous sermon "By Grace Ye Are Saved through Faith." This became the theme of his life thereafter.

Wesley immediately left for Germany, where he visited the Moravian Brethren leader Count Zinzendorf. He returned to England in September 1738, joining Charles in preaching the gospel wherever they were permitted. The Anglican congregations soon closed their doors to the Wesleys because of their enthusiasm, but they were invited to the religious societies that existed within the Church of England. In May 1738 they had founded their own "little society" on Fetter Lane, London. By autumn the Fetter Lane society numbered fifty-six men and eight women.

Encouraged by the Great Awakening in New England and by George Whitefield's successes at outdoor preaching, Wesley began preaching in fields at Bristol (1739). This sparked the great Methodist revival in England. During the following fifty years, John Wesley rode 250,000 miles on the roads of England, Scotland, and Ireland to preach 42,000 sermons. He also published 233 books. His tireless and incessant activity changed the face of British society forever.

In 1739 Wesley bought and renovated an abandoned cannon foundry near London. Seating fifteen hundred, the foundry served as Methodist headquarters for thirty-eight years until, in 1777, City Road Chapel was built.

John Wesley's unique, practical genius can be seen in his ability to organize. Wesley's Methodist societies stand as a testament to his work in evangelism. He published *Rules* for the Methodist societies in 1743 to avoid the scandal of unworthy members. In 1744 the societies imitated the early church in holding love feasts and broke new ground by gathering in the first annual conference. This gathering of preachers at Wesley's invitation developed into a sort of parliament, deciding doctrinal and administrative questions. The conference perpetuated Wesley's authority among the British Methodists after his death.

The Methodist Revival caused a great tumult in England. Rioting mobs often threatened the lives of Wesley and his followers. Methodism eventually emerged as an evangelical order within the Church of England, though it was never appreciated or approved by the church hierarchy. Church doors continued to be closed to Wesley's teaching. Nevertheless, Wesley was a member of the Church of England until his death. He refused to schedule Methodist meetings to conflict with Anglican services.

Wesley broke the mold of the settled Anglican curate and became an extensively itinerant preacher. Most ordained clergymen of the day had no taste for this approach to the ministry. So Wesley was forced to enlist a band of dedicated lay workers who also became itinerant preachers and administrators of the Methodist societies. These Methodist "circuit riders" became an important element in American life after the American Revolution.

In 1770 Wesley sent Francis Asbury to America to strengthen and enlarge the societies there, and in 1772 Wesley ordained Thomas Coke as general superintendent of the Methodists in America. Coke then ordained Asbury. This development horrified

Charles, who said that his brother had "assumed the episcopal character." John later ordained several others "to administer the sacraments of baptism and the Lord's Supper according to the usage of the Church of England." Yet Wesley continued to hold that Methodism was simply a society of Christians who would remain loyal to their own church or denomination.

John Wesley's tireless work did reap some negative consequences, however. His marriage suffered as a result of his busy lifestyle, and his wife, Maria, resented the regimen he followed in his work. In 1771 she left without warning. Attempts at reconciliation were made, but when his wife was buried on October 12, 1781, John had not even heard of her death.

Among Wesley's many books were educational treatises, translations from Greek, Latin, and Hebrew, histories of Rome and England, an ecclesiastical history, and biblical commentaries. He edited *Imitation of Christ* and works by Bunyan, Baxter, Edwards, Rutherford, and Law. He compiled an English dictionary, published twenty-three collections of hymns, and recorded his activities, travels, and spiritual life in his *Journal* (1735–1790). His medical handbook, *Primitive Physick,* went through twenty-three editions in his lifetime and nine after his death.

Beginning in the days of the Holy Club and until his death, Wesley was concerned "to reform the nation." He pioneered or participated in many causes of his day: legal and prison reform, civil rights, popular education, and abolition of slavery. Wesley's last act was to dictate a letter to William Wilberforce, who was fighting in Parliament to abolish the slave trade.

At ten o'clock on Wednesday morning, March 2, 1791, John Wesley passed into eternity. Thousands filed by his open coffin in City Road Chapel. Memorial services were held throughout England, Scotland, and Ireland; and newspapers and magazines published scores of sermons and articles. At the funeral John Whitehead echoed the hearts of millions of mourners as he lamented, "Know ye not that there is a prince and a great man fallen this day in Israel?" (2 Samuel 3:38, KJV).

John Wesley's *Journal* has been collected into eight large volumes. In it are found his thoughts and experiences on a wide variety of topics, revealing the practical devotional life of a great Christian leader.

In his *Journal* Wesley writes freely of his various experiences. He recorded the story of his conversion at a meeting on Aldersgate Street, London. He reveals his experience and dependence on the presence of God in everyday life. He describes his understanding of faith as one of the gifts of the Spirit and asserts that a person must "have some degree of it before all things in him are become new" (December 31, 1739). Wesley details his experiences with the gift of healing and often describes various miracles and prophecies.

Wesley's *Journal* chronicles how his spirituality evidenced itself in practical approaches to social concerns. He addressed such topics as tax paying, conscription, slavery, and the American Revolution. He was always concerned with employing the poor. Wesley also testified to his pioneering role in advocating the education of children.

From his experience at Aldersgate, Wesley never ceased to advocate the fullness of life in Christ. He continually struggled to desire heavenly reward rather than earthly riches. And so John Wesley's heart still influences others through his personal *Journal.*

◆ Wesley, John. *The Journal of John Wesley.* Edited by Elisabeth Jay. New York: Oxford University Press, 1987.

The Early
Twentieth Century

........*How to Pray* 1900
R. A. Torrey (1856–1928)

Reuben Archer Torrey was born to a wealthy family in Hoboken, New Jersey. Financial well-being combined with a strong body and mind guaranteed the boy a bright future. Despite his mother's desire that he enter the ministry, R. A. Torrey matriculated at Yale University in New Haven, Connecticut, to pursue a career in law. At the end of his junior year, a series of disappointments made him despondent. So he prayed, "God, if you will take away this awful burden, I will preach." This prayer brought him peace. He later recounted, "Though I had gotten over sermons and arguments and churches, and everything else, I could not get over my mother's prayers."

After his undergraduate work, Torrey completed his seminary studies at Yale Divinity School and was ordained a Congregational minister in 1883. He held various pastorates and studied abroad. In 1889 he was asked by D. L. Moody to organize and direct a new Bible school in Chicago—the Institute of the Chicago Evangelistic Society, now the Moody Bible Institute. He served as the superintendent of the Institute until 1908. From

1894 to 1906, Torrey served also as pastor of the Chicago Avenue Church (now Moody Memorial Church).

Like Moody, Torrey practiced mass evangelism. With Charles M. Alexander as his song leader, Torrey conducted a remarkable series of tours to Australia, New Zealand, India, China, Japan, Germany, Great Britain, Canada, and elsewhere. In Australia, Torrey was known as "the man with God aback of him."

These tours continued until 1911. The next year Torrey became the head of the newly formed Bible Institute of Los Angeles (Biola). Like his work at Moody Bible Institute, Torrey's leadership built the foundation for this important institution. While in Los Angles he was also pastor of the downtown Church of the Open Door.

R. A. Torrey produced a large number of written works notable for their opposition to Protestant liberalism. He advocated highly conservative doctrine and practice in such titles as *What the Bible Teaches; The Holy Spirit: Who He Is, and What He Does; Why I Believe the Bible to Be the Word of God;* and *How to Work for Christ.*

Torrey was also one of the compilers of *The Fundamentals,* a periodical published from 1910 to 1915, whose title gave rise to the term *fundamentalist.* Here he published many articles expounding conservative Protestantism.

The first chapter of *How to Pray* is titled "The Importance of Prayer." It begins with a shout:

> In Ephesians 6:18 (KJV) we read words which put the tremendous importance of prayer with startling and overwhelming force: "Praying always with all prayer and supplication in the Spirit, and watching thereunto with all perseverance and supplication for all saints." Note the *all*s: "with all prayer," . . . "in all perseverance," "for all the saints." Note once more the strong expression, "Watching

thereunto," more literally, "being sleepless thereunto."
. . . I wish that these words . . . might burn into our hearts.
I wish the whole verse might burn into our hearts.

Torrey continues by posing a question: "Why is this constant,
persistent, sleepless, overcoming prayer so needful?" The
remainder of the first chapter is the author's answer in ten short
sections. Torrey asserts that prayer is God's appointed way for
obtaining things, and the great secret of all lack in our life and
work is neglect of prayer; prayer occupied a very prominent
place and played a very important part in the earthly life of our
Lord; and prayer is the means that God has appointed for our
receiving mercy and obtaining grace to help in time of need.
Torrey advises:

> Who is there that does not feel that he needs more grace?
> Then ask for it. Be constant and persistent in your asking.
> Be importunate and untiring in your asking. God delights
> to have us "shameless" beggars in this direction; for it
> shows our faith in him, and he is mightily pleased with
> faith. Because of our "shamelessness" he will rise and give
> us as much as we need (Luke 11:8). What little streams of
> mercy and grace most of us know, when we might know
> rivers overflowing their banks!

The remaining eleven chapters of this small book describe the
principles of effective prayer according to Scripture. Composed
in a simple outline form and with easy-to-understand language,
the discussion includes such concepts as the one to whom we
pray, the necessity of obedience, the name of Christ and the will
of God, prayer in the Spirit; abiding in Christ, thanksgiving,
hindrances to prayer, when to pray, and more.

Torrey does not, however, teach dry methods for prayer but
rather practical pointers that clearly reveal the conditions God

has established for intelligent, effective prayer. In *How to Pray* the reader may find the true spirit of prayer that is found in a heart aligned with God's will.

◆ Torrey, R. A. *How to Pray.* Chicago: Moody Press, 1989.

▸ . . . . *Practical Mysticism* **1914**
    Evelyn Underhill (1875-1941)

Evelyn Underhill was born in London, the only child of Sir Arthur Underhill, a distinguished lawyer and enthusiastic yachtsman. Raised an Anglican and educated at King's College for Women in London, she showed interest in writing fiction, though her first book was a work of humorous verse. As a girl, Underhill began annual trips to the continent with her parents and was charmed by Paris, Chartres, Florence, and Rome. She had many interests: cats, sailing, bookbinding, archaeology, bicycling, flowers, birds, gardening. In 1907 she began to write *Mysticism: A Study in the Nature and Development of Man's Spiritual Consciousness.* Published in 1911, this classic work is a superb evaluation of spirituality from the early Christian era to the beginning of the twentieth century.

Underhill was a prolific writer on the spiritual life, a sensible and encouraging spiritual director, a promoter of the retreat movement, and highly influential in the Anglican tradition. She was a woman whose own spiritual journey was long and painful, but while mixing mysticism with common sense, she helped many to grow in faith. In 1907 she was married to Hubert Stuart Moore, also a yachtsman. In 1911 she began her friendship with Baron Friedrich von Hügel, with whom she corresponded extensively and who exercised a strong influence upon her spiritual life, especially between 1921 and the time of his death in 1925. Though Underhill was impressed with Roman

Catholicism, she remained an Anglican, giving herself to social services, speaking at church retreats, and writing. She was the first woman to be chosen by any Oxford college as an outside lecturer on religion.

A combination of a good ethical life with a deep sense of devotion to God, Underhill's life was an example of practical mysticism. To her the life of a religious person was not one estranged in a monastery but one concerned with the problems of everyday living, especially with the poor, to which she gave two afternoons a week working in the slums at North Kensington during a portion of her life.

In addition to *Mysticism,* Underhill's other writings on the devotional life are *The Mystic Way* (1913), *Practical Mysticism* (1914), and *The Essentials of Mysticism* (1920). Her much-praised work *Worship* (1937) is a study in liturgical practices in various church traditions.

Practical Mysticism, given the descriptive subtitle *A Little Book for Normal People* in the original edition, deals with Christian mysticism, contemplation, and the meaning of the mystical life. In it Evelyn Underhill writes engagingly to invite the reader to the possibilities of growing deeper in relationship with Reality, that is: the God of the Universe. Referring to Ephesians 3:18 and quoting Acts 17:28, she says:

> Because mystery is horrible to us, we have agreed for
> the most part to live in a world of labels; to make of them
> the current coin of experience, and ignore their merely
> symbolic character, the infinite gradation of values which
> they misrepresent. We simply do not attempt to unite
> with Reality. But now and then that symbolic character
> is suddenly brought home to us. Some great emotion, so
> devastating visitation of beauty, love or pain, lifts us to
> another level of consciousness; and we are aware for a

moment of the difference between the neat collection of discrete objects and experiences which we call the world and the height, the depth, the breadth of the living growing, changing Fact, of which thought, life, and energy are parts and in which we "live and move and have our being."

Thomas Kepler wrote of Underhill: "No woman in Christian history has written more on the meaning and value of Christian mysticism; and few have been able to interpret the meaning of mysticism in terms of practical, everyday living in a deeper fashion." In her writing Underhill emphasized a complete trust in God. "Lord help me to trust you through thick and thin," she prayed. Seeking to establish the uniqueness of Christianity, she wrote: "In the depth of reality revealed by the cross, Christianity stands alone," but her approach to personal religious experience had much in common with other faiths besides the Anglican, and *Worship* expresses a deeply ecumenical approach to liturgical worship.

In *Practical Mysticism* Underhill is down-to-earth, concrete, and sensible. But she writes with an attractive energy and enthusiasm. The reader wants to be part of the holy adventure of mysticism and desires a profound relationship with God. The book's short and easy-to-read chapters are titled "What is Mysticism?"; "The World of Reality"; "The Preparation of the Mystic"; "Meditation and Recollection"; "Self-Adjustment"; "Love and Will"; "The First, Second, and Third forms of Contemplation"; and "The Mystical Life."

In *Immanence: A Book of Verses* (1912) Evelyn Underhill illustrates how, to her, the practical and ordinary are also mystical:

I come in the little things, saith the Lord. . . .

◆ Underhill, Evelyn. *Practical Mysticism.* Alpharetta, Ga.: Ariel Press, 1988.

.... *Leaves from the Notebooks of a Tamed Cynic* **1929**
Reinhold Niebuhr (1892–1971)

Reinhold Niebuhr was born in Wright City, Missouri. In 1902, at the age of ten, Niebuhr decided that he wanted to emulate his father and become a minister. So he attended Elmhurst College in 1910 and Eden Theological Seminary from 1910 to 1913. He also pursued graduate work at Yale University.

Niebuhr was ordained into the ministry of the Evangelical Synod of North America (now part of the United Church of Christ) in 1915 and was pastor of Bethel Evangelical Church, Detroit, Michigan, from 1915 to 1928. It was there that Niebuhr came of age theologically as his liberalism faced the harsh, dehumanizing realities of industrial America. He became upset with what industrial life did to the laborers and wondered what hope there was for American civilization when "naïve gentlemen with a genius for mechanics suddenly become the arbiters over the lives and fortunes of hundreds of thousands."

In *Leaves from the Notebooks of a Tamed Cynic,* Niebuhr records his thoughts after a tour of an automobile factory in 1925:

> The men seemed weary. . . . Their sweat and their dull pain are part of the price paid for the fine cars we all run. . . .
> We are all responsible. We all want the things which the factory produces, and none of us is sensitive enough to care how much in human values the efficiency of the modern factory costs. Beside the brutal facts of modern industrial life, how futile are all our homiletical spoutings! The church is undoubtedly cultivating graces and preserving spiritual amenities in the more protected areas of society. But it isn't changing the essential facts of modern industrial civilization by a hair's breadth. It isn't even thinking about them.

Niebuhr's experience in Detroit was also crucial in the formation of his political outlook. He identified with liberal causes while remaining anti-Communist and sharply critical of totalitarianism. While still in Detroit, Niebuhr began to advocate radical solutions to the human crisis as he saw it—socialism and pacifism for life in society, a new "Christian realism" for theology.

In 1928 Niebuhr joined the faculty of Union Theological Seminary in New York, where he held various positions, including William E. Dodge Jr. Professor of Applied Christianity, Charles A. Briggs Graduate Professor of Ethics and Theology, and vice president of the seminary, 1955–1960. He was a founder of Americans for Democratic Action, cofounder of Fellowship of Socialist Christians, and was a research associate for the Institute of War and Peace Studies, Columbia University.

In 1960 a professorship was established and funded in his honor at Union Theological Seminary by a cross-denominational group including Jacques Maritain, T. S. Eliot, Arnold Toynbee, and Eleanor Roosevelt.

Niebuhr had an acute intellect and an encyclopedic knowledge. His extensive theological influence and lifelong attempt to integrate Christian ethics with practical political philosophy won him an audience among influential secularists, including George F. Kennan, Arthur Schlesinger Jr., Dean Acheson, McGeorge Bundy, Hans J. Morgenthau, and James Reston. Niebuhr's philosophy, described as socialist, liberal, and pragmatist in politics, and conservative, neoorthodox, and realist in theology, reflected his belief in the necessity for a complex explanation of reality.

In theology, Niebuhr combined the perspectives of Augustine, Luther, and Calvin. He held the traditional Christian view of humanity flawed by the effects of original sin. As a result Niebuhr disagreed with liberal Protestantism, regarding it as utopian. Niebuhr rejected what he saw as the two extremes of Protestantism: One sought total withdrawal from the secular order, the other sought total immersion into the affairs of the world through the social gospel. His philosophy of Christian realism was an attempt to strike a middle course between the two, with a political philosophy built on the foundation of a vigorous and consistent Christianity.

Reinhold Niebuhr systematically developed his theological ethics in a long list of major books. The two most important are *Moral Man and Immoral Society* (1932) and *The Nature and Destiny of Man* (1941, 1943). The first severely criticized the liberal optimism concerning humanity. It pointed out that social groups are selfish almost by their very definition. It gave a sharp rebuke to the notion that human beings are perfectible as individuals and inherently good in groups.

The second provided a more systematic discussion of what Niebuhr called mankind's "most vexing problem. How shall he think of himself?" In this work and elsewhere Niebuhr proposed to answer his own question: man as sinner and saint, man as subject to history and social forces but also as shaper of history and society, man as creature of the Creator but potential lord of the creation, man as egotistical but capable of living for others.

In the person of Christ, Niebuhr found a unique example of an individual who used power only for good and not—as all other people—for evil. The cross of Christ was a particularly important theme for Niebuhr, since it revealed the great paradox of powerlessness turned into power.

Will Herberg, a Jewish theologian, once said: "No Protestant theologian has spoken so relevantly to our concerns in the Western world as has Reinhold Niebuhr. . . . [He is] one of the most creative and influential minds of our generation."

Niebuhr, however, was not confined to theory. For most of his life he was deeply involved in political concerns on a practical level. In 1930 he ran unsuccessfully on the Socialist ticket for Congress in New York and was involved in various pacifist causes until the Nazi occupation of the Rhineland in 1936. At that time he urged U.S. intervention on behalf of the Allies. Niebuhr viewed the expansionist policies of Hitler as profoundly anti-Christian.

Niebuhr lectured and preached widely. He criticized the secular world and also Christians for what he saw as a misunderstanding of Christianity. He wrote: "If faith produces fanatic fury rather than charity, it becomes as sounding brass and a tinkling cymbal."

Leaves from the Notebooks of a Tamed Cynic is a record of Reinhold Niebuhr's years in active ministry in Detroit. Its entries date from 1915 to 1928. Concerning *Leaves* Niebuhr writes: "The notes which have been chosen for publication have been picked to illustrate the typical problem of a modern minister in an industrial and urban community and what seem to be more or less typical reactions of a young minister to such problems." The first entry begins, "There is something ludicrous about a callow young fool like myself standing up to preach a sermon to these good folks. I talk wisely about life and know little about life's problems." The second entry begins, "I am glad there are only eighteen families in this church. I have been visiting the members for six weeks and haven't seen all of them yet."

In his 1956 introduction Niebuhr admits that his observations of thirty years previous appear to be dated. So now, several decades later, a reader may think that Niebuhr's reflections are in some ways quaint. But they are much more. Frank, candid, searching, shrewd, incisive, humble, and beautifully sincere—these are descriptions of the book by reviewers of the time.

The following is his observation after sitting in on another man's sermon:

> Throughout the whole discourse there ran the erroneous assumption that Christians are real followers of Jesus and no effort was made to describe the wide chasm which

yawns between the uncompromising idealism of the Galilean and the current morality. . . . How much easier it is to adore an ideal character than to emulate it.

Niebuhr's criticism and concern for the relevance of theology to the political and social situation of the modern world was significantly shaped by his experience as a young minister in Detroit. *Leaves from the Notebooks of a Tamed Cynic* is a small, simple book in comparison with the author's later writing, yet it gives precious and inspiring insight into the heart of Reinhold Niebuhr at the beginning of his career.

At the end of that career *The Christian Century* observed:

Reinhold Niebuhr was as conscious as any modern man that he faces the eternal in every moment and in every action of his life. No man brooded more than he over the limitations of all historical achievements nor was more persuaded of the power of faith to transcend those limitations. No man has been better prepared in mind to confront the end of history that is death's own promise.

◆ Niebuhr, Reinhold. *Leaves from the Notebooks of a Tamed Cynic.* Louisville, Ky.: Westminster John Knox Press, 1990.

........*My Utmost for His Highest* 1935
Oswald Chambers (1874–1917)

Oswald Chambers was born the son of a Baptist preacher in Aberdeen, Scotland. He became a believer in Christ through the preaching of Charles Spurgeon and abandoned a promising career in art to train for the Baptist ministry at Dunoon College.

Most of the public ministry of Oswald Chambers was with the Pentecostal League of Prayer, especially after the league's founder died in 1909. Chambers visited Holiness camps in the

United States and Japan before becoming principal of the Bible Training College in London. With his wife, Gertrude, he ministered to British troops in Egypt. It was here that a sudden illness took his life.

More than forty titles of Chambers's works have been published posthumously, the most popular being *My Utmost for His Highest*. This is the most widely read book of its kind. Compiled by his wife from her notes of his sermons in London and Egypt, *My Utmost* was published in 1935. Since then it has sold millions of copies and is still enjoyed today. A popular edition with carefully updated terminology and language has also recently been published.

In her introduction, Gertrude Chambers tells of the sources of the readings in *My Utmost*:

> These daily readings have been selected from various sources, chiefly from the lectures given at the Bible Training College, Clapham, during the years 1911–1915; then, from October 1915 to November 1917, from talks given night by night in the YMCA Huts, Zeitoun, Egypt.

My Utmost for His Highest consists of 365 readings, each assigned a date from January 1 through December 31. Each reading bears its own title and begins with a verse of Scripture. Chambers then addresses a topic related to the verse of the day. Verses are selected from almost every New Testament book, and many come from the Old Testament as well. In the Old Testament Chambers quotes mostly from Genesis, Psalms, and Isaiah. In the New Testament, special attention is given to the Gospels of Matthew and John, with seventy-two readings taken from the Gospel of John alone.

The subjects covered in *My Utmost* span a wide range of spiritual and practical concerns. These include drudgery, friendship with God, introspection, laziness, and moods. Redemption is discussed in twenty-two readings, and spiritual ambition is covered in over fifty.

Following is a sample of the reading for January 1 (Philippians 1:20). It explains Chamber's concept "my utmost for His Highest":

> Paul says—"My determination is to be my utmost for His Highest." To get there is a question of will, not of debate nor of reasoning, but a surrender of will, an absolute and irrevocable surrender on that point. An overweening consideration for ourselves is the thing that keeps us from that decision, though we put it that we are considering others. When we consider what it will cost others if we obey the call of Jesus, we tell God He does not know what our obedience will mean. Keep to the point; He does know. Shut out every other consideration and keep yourself before God for this one thing only—my utmost for His Highest. I am determined to be absolutely and entirely for Him and for Him alone.

♦ Chambers, Oswald. *My Utmost for His Highest.* Uhrichsville, Ohio: Barbour Publishing, 1998.

♦ Chambers, Oswald. *My Utmost for His Highest: An Updated Edition in Today's Language.* Edited by James Reimann. Grand Rapids: Discovery House, 1992.

. . . . *A Dairy of Private Prayer* 1936
John Baillie (1886–1960)

The Scottish theologian, educator, and ecumenical leader John Baillie was born in Gairloch, Scotland, and educated at Edinburgh, Jena, and Marburg universities. He was brother to Donald MacPherson Baillie (1877–1954), whose *God Was in Christ* (1947) has been described as one of the most original treatments of Christology in modern theology. These two were keenly interested in the ecumenical movement, particularly its Faith and Order branch. Baillie served with the YMCA in World War I after which he became professor of theology at Auburn Seminary, New York (1919–1927). He then taught at Emmanuel College, Toronto (1927–1930), and Union Seminary, New York (1930–1934). He occupied the chair of divinity at Edinburgh University, Scotland, until his retirement in 1956.

But Baillie was more than an academic or theologian. During World War II he served the Church of Scotland as chairman of a commission appointed "for the interpretation of the will of God in the present crisis." He was elected to the central committee of the World Council of Churches at its first assembly in 1948.

Plus, Baillie wrote on many aspects of the Christian faith. His best-known works are *And the Life Everlasting* (1934), *The Sense of the Presence of God,* and the devotional classic *A Diary of Private Prayer* (1936). The latter book has remained in print to this day with over one million books sold.

A Diary of Private Prayer is a small prayer book composed of two daily prayers, morning and evening, for thirty-one days. The author's note describes the book in this way:

> Here are prayers for all the mornings and evenings of the months; and at the end of the book two prayers which, when any day falls on a Sunday, may be substituted for the others or else added to them. These prayers are to be regarded as aids; they are not intended to form the whole of the morning's or evening's devotions or to take the place of more individual prayers for oneself and others. On the blank left-hand pages such further petitions and intercessions may be noted down.
>
> The prayers are suited to private use, not to the liturgical use of public worship.

Baillie's prayers are wonderfully rich; they encompass much of the human heart and need; they address God with an all-inclusive vision of the divine person. Founded on Scripture and theologically sound, each prayer is two hundred to three hundred words in length. The use of this small book provides a believer with eloquence he or she may not naturally possess. Bible quotations and lists give expression to one's longing, hope, and need. God's love, Christ's life, human shortcomings, and the needs of others are themes that are often repeated. Here is a portion of the morning prayer for the first day:

> Eternal father of my soul, let my first thought today be of Thee, let my first impulse be to worship Thee, let my first speech be Thy name, let my first action be to kneel before Thee in prayer.
>
> For Thy perfect wisdom and perfect goodness:
> For the love wherewith Thou lovest mankind:
> For the love wherewith Thou lovest me:
> For the great and mysterious opportunity of my life:
> For the indwelling of Thy Spirit in my heart:
> For the sevenfold gifts of Thy Spirit:
> I praise and worship Thee, O Lord.

This classic book of prayer and devotion is useful for a month or for consecutive months through the year. It enlarges the believer's vocabulary of prayer, turns the mind to subjects that may be unattended, and enriches the understanding of the power and love of God.

◆ Baillie, John. *A Diary of Private Prayer*. New York: Simon and Schuster, 1996.

The Cost of Discipleship 1937
Dietrich Bonhoeffer (1906–1944)

Dietrich Bonhoeffer was born in Breslau (now Wroclaw, Poland). His father was the foremost neurologist and psychiatrist teaching at the University of Berlin; his mother was the grand-daughter of Karl von Hase, a nineteenth-century church historian. At the age of seventeen, Bonhoeffer began theological studies at Tübingen. He also enrolled at the University of Berlin for additional theological studies. At the age of twenty-four, Bonhoeffer began to teach at the University of Berlin.

While studying at Union Theological Seminary in New York City (1930–1931), Bonhoeffer team-taught a Sunday school class at a church in Harlem. This experience proved to be a powerful lesson for the young man about how "enslaved" people could endure dehumanizing oppression by exercising simple, biblical faith, particularly in praise and worship.

Bonhoeffer returned to Germany, and when many pastors were yielding to Hitler's interference in church affairs, he resisted and helped create the Confessing Church in Germany. In February 1933, Bonhoeffer delivered a lecture broadcast over Berlin radio in which he told the public that they desired a leader who would inevitably become a "misleader" because of his desire to become the idol of those he led. The broadcast was cut off before he finished. When Hitler became chancellor of Germany, Bonhoeffer took work as a pastor in London. In 1935 he returned at the request of the Confessing Church to found and lead an illegal seminary in Finkenwalde.

From the earliest days of the Nazi regime, Bonhoeffer identified with the resistance movement against Adolf Hitler, who in 1933 had become the dictator of Germany. On November 9, 1938, Bonhoeffer witnessed *Kristallnacht,* when over six hundred synagogues were destroyed, seventy-five hundred Jewish shops were looted, and thirty-five thousand Jews were arrested. This led Bonhoeffer and other conspirators to intensify their efforts against the Nazi regime; they plotted to kill Hitler in order to end Nazi power. Bonhoeffer was eventually arrested in April 1943 and hanged in 1944, shortly after the plot to kill Hitler failed.

Published in 1937, *The Cost of Discipleship* reaffirms the concept of faith in a Christian's life. Bonhoeffer emphasizes the Word (the Scriptures), the sacraments (baptism and the Lord's Supper), and the earthly community of faith (the church). The book's title in German is simply *Discipleship*. Bonhoeffer takes the pillars of reformed theology (faith, justification, and sanctification) and unites them into the single concept of discipleship.

Here is the key formula of this work: "Only he who believes is obedient, and only he who is obedient believes." Bonhoeffer claims that this idea validates justification and restores its true value. But Bonhoeffer emphasizes the community of faith as well. In *The Cost of Discipleship,* Bonhoeffer insists that it is impossible to become a new person as a solitary individual. "It means the church, the body of Christ, in fact it means Christ himself."

But he is not advocating a world movement or creed. Nor is discipleship an ideology or technique. These require measurable results. Rather, Bonhoeffer says that correct Christology requires that a person be called and then follow. Those who do this "are ready to suffer with the Word."

The Cost of Discipleship is divided into four chapters. The opening chapter challenges the reader with a discourse on grace and discipleship. Bonhoeffer attacks the "cheap grace" that was being preached in the churches of his time. He counters this, saying, "When Christ calls a man, he bids him come and die."

Chapter 2 further develops Bonhoeffer's discussion of discipleship as it examines Jesus Christ's demands on the believer in the Sermon on the Mount. Chapter 3 discusses spreading this message of Jesus Christ, and chapter 4 addresses the believer and his or her relationship to the church, the body of Christ on earth.

In this classic work, Bonhoeffer describes a disciple's life as simple and carefree. This simplicity is rooted in the disciple's obedience to one master, which sets the disciple free from other concerns. The truth of this work is reinforced by the real-life example of Bonhoeffer himself. He writes:

> The call of Jesus makes the disciple community not only the salt but also the light of the world: their activity is visible, as well as imperceptible. "You *are* the light." Once again it is not: "you are to be the light," they are already the light because Christ has called them. They are a light which is seen of me, they cannot be otherwise, and if they were it would be a sign that they had not been called. How impossible, how utterly absurd it would be for the disciples— *these* disciples, such men as these!—to try and *become* the light of the world! No. They are already the light and the call has made them so. Nor does Jesus say: "You have the light." The light is not an instrument which has been put into their hands, such as their preaching. It is the disciples themselves.

♦ Bonhoeffer, Dietrich. *The Cost of Discipleship*. New York: Simon and Schuster, 1976.

The Later
Twentieth Century

.... *Mere Christianity* **1952**
C. S. Lewis (1898–1962)

Born in Belfast, Ireland, C. S. Lewis grew up in the Anglican Church but became an atheist in his teenage years—an unpromising beginning for the man who would become one of the most important Christian thinkers of the twentieth century. Lewis attended Oxford University, where his studies were interrupted by military service in World War I. Returning to Oxford he became a fellow of Magdalen College, where he remained for nearly thirty years. Lewis moved from atheism to theism to Christianity and became a Christian at about age thirty. Shortly afterward he wrote his autobiographical novel, *The Pilgrim's Regress* (1933). His first scholarly work, *The Allegory of Love,* appeared in 1936.

Lewis's newfound faith created a torrent of writing during his years at Oxford. For a long time *The Screwtape Letters* (1942) was his most popular work. Lewis wrote this book as a collection of letters from a major devil to a lesser one in charge of a young man's soul. He also wrote *The Problem of Pain* (1940), *Abolition of Man* (1943), *Miracles* (1947), the Space Trilogy (1938–1945), and *Mere Christianity* (1952), the simple but profound apologetic for Christianity.

In 1954 Lewis accepted the newly created chair of Medieval and Renaissance English at Cambridge University. The same year his best-known scholarly work, *English Literature in the Sixteenth Century,* was published. Lewis told of his upbringing and conversion in *Surprised by Joy* (1955) and published a fictional series for children called the Chronicles of Narnia (1950–1956).

In 1956 Lewis married Joy Davidman Gresham, an American Jewish-Christian who was very ill with cancer. Four years later she died, and Lewis recorded his mourning in *A Grief Observed.*

C. S. Lewis's twenty-five books have sold millions of copies over the years, and several literary societies have been formed in his honor. His combination of sound reasoning, interesting imagery, and understandable language appeal to countless readers. His works are classic favorites for millions.

In the early 1940s C. S. Lewis delivered a series of broadcasts, which were published as *The Case for Christianity* (1943), *Christian Behaviour* (1943), and *Beyond Personality* (1945). Years later these works were gathered together as *Mere Christianity* (1952). In his preface to *Mere Christianity,* Lewis relates his purpose: "I have thought that the best . . . service I could do for my unbelieving neighbours was to explain and defend the belief that has been common to nearly all Christians at all times." It is this that he calls "mere" Christianity.

Book 1 of *Mere Christianity* is titled *Right and Wrong as a Clue to the Meaning of the Universe.* Its five chapters cover the problems of right and wrong behavior, moral law versus instinct, the power that gives force to the law, and the absolute goodness behind moral law. It is at this point that, as Lewis says, "Christianity begins to talk."

Book 2 is titled *What Christians Believe.* Here Lewis first addresses atheism, pantheism, and the Christian idea of God.

He then discusses the rebellion of Satan, calling Christianity "the story of how the rightful king has landed" on enemy territory. Concerning Jesus Christ, Lewis challenges the reader to consider the following: "A man who was merely a man and said the sort of things Jesus said would not be a great moral teacher. He would either be a lunatic . . . or else he would be the Devil of Hell. You must make your choice." Lewis also discusses the atonement and Christ's nature as both divine and human.

Christian Behaviour is the title of Book 3. He analyzes the three parts of morality: harmony between individuals, harmony within the individual, and the general purpose of human life. One chapter is devoted to the cardinal or "pivotal" virtues: prudence, temperance, justice, and fortitude. Another covers the New Testament's description of a fully Christian society. Other chapters address psychoanalysis, sexuality, and marriage. Book 3 closes with discussions about forgiveness, loving your neighbor, pride, and the three "theological virtues" of charity, hope, and faith.

The fourth and final book, *Beyond Personality: or First Steps on the Doctrine of the Trinity,* contains eleven short chapters. Here Lewis discusses theology and refers to it as a "map" of Christianity. Lewis's theological map charts several things: natural human life, spiritual life, the Trinity, time and eternity, the Incarnation, and the meaning of several New Testament phrases, such as "born again" and "be ye perfect."

As devotional literature *Mere Christianity* is both comforting and challenging. The following is a comment concerning the beginning of a Christian's day:

> The real problem of the Christian life comes where people do not usually look for it. It comes the very moment you wake up each morning. All your wishes and hopes for the day rush at you like wild animals. And the first job each morning consists simply in shoving them all back; in listen-

ing to that other voice, taking that other point of view, letting that other larger, stronger, quieter life come flowing in. And so on, all day. Standing back from all your natural fussings and frettings; coming in out of the wind.

In *Mere Christianity* C. S. Lewis explains the Christian faith without making direct reference to a single verse of the New Testament. This helps to make the book very understandable for new Christians and unbelievers, who may not be familiar with the Bible.

Lewis closes his classic by encouraging the reader to "look for Christ and you will find Him, and with Him everything else thrown in."

♦ Lewis, C. S. *Mere Christianity*. New York: Simon and Schuster, 1996.

The Prayers of Kierkegaard 1956
Søren Kierkegaard (1813–1855)

Søren Kierkegaard, the Danish philosopher and religious thinker, was born in Copenhagen. He was the youngest of seven children and raised by a melancholic and devoutly religious father who stressed the suffering of Christ in his children's upbringing.

Kierkegaard studied philosophy and theology at the University of Copenhagen. There his personal despair grew. This resulted in his decision to become a cleric and marry his fiancée Regine Olsen, the daughter of a treasury official. But after completing his doctoral dissertation, *The Concept of Irony* (1841), he broke the engagement. Then Kierkegaard began a life of seclusion as a writer and produced a constant flow of books with at least twelve major philosophical essays over the next ten years.

Kierkegaard's early philosophical works appeared under pseudonyms. In *Either/Or* (1843) he wrote of two ways of life, the first being the temporal "aesthetic," based on intellectual or physical sensory pleasures. This way leads to "dread" *(angst),* the call of the infinite, and eventually despair. The second way is the "ethical," based in moral codes and the infinite, the eternal. This work startled the religious world with its denouncement of Christianity.

Kierkegaard's work was designed to challenge the institutional church. He saw that the church had removed two necessary elements in the Christian's life—faith and commitment to God. He said the church had minimized the distance between the human and the divine. But Kierkegaard saw a great chasm between God and human beings. The only bridge of this abyss is Jesus Christ.

Also in 1843 he wrote *Fear and Trembling,* which deals with the conflict between the ethical and the religious. This is shown in Abraham's decision to sacrifice his son in obedience to God's command. Abraham got his son back after proving his faith, showing that with God anything is possible—one can be forced to disregard ethics if God commands it. This is the paradoxical nature of religion. So God can accomplish what to the human mind is absurd, and by having faith in the absurd, one can recover what was lost.

Next Kierkegaard wrote *Philosophical Fragments* (1844), in which he attempts to present Christianity as it should be. Continuing the theme of the paradox, he says that Christ is the absolute paradox—God in time, both infinite and finite—that humans cannot comprehend. God is infinitely higher than man, because man lives in sin, and therefore God always appears paradoxical. And so Christianity seems absurd.

Then came *Stages on Life's Way* (1845). Here the author states that there are three spheres, or stages, of human life. This is the sequel of *Either/Or.* In it he adds a third stage to the aesthetic and the ethical—the religious. The ethical is a transition stage because its laws are impossible to fulfill. One must believe in the paradox of God in Christ and enter the religious, the fulfillment.

Concluding Unscientific Postscript (1846) attacks Hegelianism because of Hegel's notion of an objective science of the human spirit that Kierkegaard thought obscured the nature of Christianity. And *Works of Love* (1847) is a description of the various kinds of love and the perfection of Christian love. Here he also writes about the "offense" of Christianity, a theme he continued in *Practice in Christianity*.

Under his own name, Kierkegaard published religious discourses—eighteen between 1843 and 1845. Publication of such discourses continued until his death. These include *Three Discourses on Imagined Occasions* (1845), *Upbuilding Discourses in Various Spirits* (1847), *Christian Discourses* (1848), *Three Discourses at the Communion On Fridays* (1849), *Two Minor Ethical-Religious Essays* (1849), and *The Changelessness of God* (1855).

The Concept of Anxiety (1844) and *The Sickness unto Death* (1849) reveal Kierkegaard's deep insights into human psychology. *The Concept of Anxiety* describes anxiety as a stage that is necessary before one makes the leap of faith into Christianity, the stage where one shudders at one's freedom. All this is considered in the context of Adam's original sin. Anxiety can lead to sin, sin compounds the anxiety of freedom, and freedom is lost through sin. This cycle of sinfulness and anxiety can be broken only by faith.

The Sickness unto Death is a brilliant description of the "self"—a synthesis of the infinite and finite, temporal and eternal, which can only find rest in God. The alternative is despair. Here he describes different kinds of despair: the despair that results from not realizing one is in despair; the despair of wishing not to be oneself; and the despair of asserting the self without relation to God. Kierkegaard concludes that despair is sin, and despair is the sickness unto death. To Kierkegaard sin and faith are opposites; either one despairs or one has faith.

Kierkegaard considered *Practice in Christianity* (1850) to be his most important book. Here he attempts to reintroduce Christianity into Christendom ("official Christianity"). This was the author's main theme until his death. He examines the offense of Christianity in a positive sense. He describes how the state church in Denmark attempted to remove this offense, thus watering down the message of the gospel. He was himself trying to be an offense, hoping this would lead Christians to a stronger faith.

In 1855, the year of his death, Kierkegaard wrote *This Must Be Said—So Let It Now Be Said* and encouraged people to leave the church because their official Christianity was a "forgery." The same year he wrote *What Christ's Judgment Is on Official Christianity,* in which he called the clergy "freethinkers" for their mediocrity.

Few nineteenth-century thinkers have surpassed Søren Kierkegaard's influence on twentieth-century thought. He strongly influenced philosophers Martin Heidegger and Jean-Paul Sartre and theologian Karl Barth and has also been admired as a literary stylist and innovator. His influence has been felt in many areas of human thought—theology, philosophy, psychology, literature, art, and biblical studies.

Perry D. LeFevre writes in his introduction to *The Prayers of Kierkegaard:* "The key to understanding Kierkegaard lies in his religious writings and in his Journals. His philosophical and aesthetic works are to be understood in the light of his religious works. It has been my intention, therefore, to take the reader to the religious center of Kierkegaard's existence. From this perspective, faith is seen to be Kierkegaard's goal, and prayer is revealed as man's sole means of moving toward that goal." So Kierkegaard prays:

> Our Father, be near to us with thy power so that we may
> feel a joyous assurance of heart that thou art not far from
> us, but that we live and move and have our being in thee.

Such prayers are found throughout the writings of Søren
Kierkegaard. LeFevre has gathered one hundred of these and
organized them in four sections: God, the Father; God, the Son;
God, the Holy Spirit; and For Special Occasions [primarily the
Lord's Table]. This collection, says LeFevre, is meant to demon-
strate "the intimate way in which Kierkegaard's own prayer
was fused with his understanding of Christian faith and life. It is
also intended to provide a rich resource of devotional material
unknown to most contemporary Christians for use in both private
and public worship."

A second part of this book is titled "An Interpretation of
Kierkegaard's Life and Thought." Divided into four sections—
His Life, Basic Themes, Toward the Christian Life, and Man
of Prayer—it reveals Kierkegaard as primarily a religious thinker.

◆ Kierkegaard, Søren. *The Prayers of Kierkegaard.* Edited by
 Perry D. LeFevre. Chicago: University of Chicago Press,
 1996.

. . . . *Hymn of the Universe* **1961**
 Pierre Teilhard de Chardin (1881–1955)

The visionary French Jesuit, geologist, paleontologist, and
philosopher-theologian, Pierre Teilhard de Chardin was noted
for his evolutionary interpretation of humanity and the universe.
He spent much of his life endeavoring to integrate religious
experience with natural science, specifically Christian theology
with theories of evolution.

Born into the family of a gentleman farmer near Clermont-

Ferrand, Teilhard joined the Jesuits when he was eighteen years of age and was ordained in 1911. Rather than serve as a chaplain in World War I, Teilhard became a stretcher bearer. He was awarded the Legion of Honour for service in the war and went on to lecture in science at the Jesuit College in Cairo. He became professor of geology at the Intitut Catholique in Paris and studied at the Institute of Human Paleontology at the Museum of Natural History in Paris.

In 1922 Teilhard received a doctorate in paleontology from the Sorbonne in Paris. A year later he embarked on a paleontological expedition to China and remained there until 1946, engaged in research in paleontology and in philosophical reflection. In 1929 Teilhard participated in the excavation that discovered Peking Man. But his unorthodox ideas caused the Jesuit order to ban his theological teaching and publishing, although his work in Cenozoic geology and paleontology became known and brought him academic distinction. Teilhard spent his final years at the Wenner-Gren Foundation, New York City, for which he made two paleontological and archaeological expeditions to South Africa.

Teilhard's major work is the posthumously published *The Phenomenon of Man* (1955). It is his attempt to develop a comprehensive evolutionary vision that simultaneously addresses scientific and religious interests. He argues that the emergence of humanity brought evolutionary development into a new dimension. Out of the layer of living things that cover the earth emerged a mind-layer—human consciousness. This generated increasingly complex social arrangements that in turn gave rise to higher consciousness. This process is continual and will culminate in the convergence of the material and the spiritual—a superconsciousness.

Today Teilhard is best known for this unique evolutionary cosmology. Some readers say that this predicted the arrival of the global Internet more than half a century before its creation. Teilhard called it the Noosphere—a global network of trade, communication, exchange of knowledge, and cooperative research weaving itself into a realm of collective thought. This evolutionary stage of humanity is a global membrane of information fueled by human consciousness. Teilhard maintained that this global network of collective minds would secure and advance the combined achievement of humanity, the only realized purpose in the universe. He wrote:

> We have reached a crossroads in human evolution where the only road which leads forward is towards a common passion. . . . To continue to place our hopes in a social order achieved by external violence would simply amount to our giving up all hope of carrying the Spirit of the Earth to its limits.

Teilhard de Chardin is unlike evolutionists who regard humanity as simply a more successful extension of Pliocene fauna. He argued that the appearance of humanity, much more than this, was the birth of reflection. . . . animals know, but a man knows that he knows. He saw human evolution presently progressing through technology, urbanization, and modern communications. Theologically, Teilhard saw human and material evolution eventually converging in God. Then will come a new order initiated by Christ's return.

In its review of *Hymn of the Universe,* the periodical *The Christian Century* wrote:

> This current volume is the most mystical and least immediately scientific of all. One need not share Teilhard's vision of the goal of history or of all the steps of development toward it in order to stand at his side and celebrate beauty and meaning in "the world of matter" where Christ is present.

This statement should come as a relief to those readers who consider that they hold a more orthodox theology than did Teilhard de Chardin. His *Hymn of the Universe* is not a scientific or theological statement of the how or why of the universe— statements Teilhard made so capably elsewhere. Rather it is a praise of the reality of the universe and its Creator. This he expresses in highly evocative poetic language that causes the reader's heart to soar in loving awe of God.

The book is composed of four sections: "The Mass on the World" is the author's well-known meditation on the Eucharistic presence of Christ through the universe—the omnipresence of the divine Word—written in 1923. The idea for this meditation occurred to Teilhard when, working in a desert in China, he had no means to celebrate the Lord's Table. The first part of "The Mass on the World" is "The Offering." Here the author writes, in part:

> Over there, on the horizon, the sun has just touched with light the outermost fringe of the eastern sky. Once again, beneath this moving sheet of fire, the living surface of the earth wakes and trembles, and once again begins its fearful travail. I will place on my paten [the plate used to hold the bread in a Eucharistic service], O God, the harvest to be won by this renewal of labor. Into my chalice I shall pour all the sap which is to be pressed out this day from the earth's fruits.

The meditation is completed in four further parts: "Fire Over The Earth," "Fire In The Earth," "Communion," and "Prayer."

The second section, titled "Christ in the World of Matter," takes the form of three stories told by a fictional friend of the author who died in the Battle of Verdun in World War I. This character, evidently a disguise for Teilhard himself, introduces the stories in this way:

> You want to know . . . how the universe, in all its power

and multiplicity, came to assume for me the lineaments of the face of Christ? This came about gradually; and it is difficult to find words in which to analyze life-renewing intuitions such as these; still, I can tell you about some of the experiences through which the light of this awareness gradually entered into my soul as though at the gradual, jerky raising of a curtain. . . .

Each brief story revolves around an object found in Roman Catholic worship and bears that name: "The Picture," "The Monstrance," and "The Pyx."

The third section of *Hymn of the Universe* is titled "The Spiritual Power of Matter"—an extended parable based on Elijah's encounter with the fiery chariot, fiery horses, and the whirlwind in 2 Kings 2:11-12. The final, largest section of the book is *"Pensées"* ("Thoughts")—a collection of eighty-one short meditations collected from Teilhard's work, published and unpublished. These are organized under four subheadings: "The Presence of God in the World," "Humanity in Progress," "The Meaning of Human Endeavor," and "In the Total Christ." Here are the final sentences of Pensée 81:

> Love certainly has in Christianity a strength which is not found elsewhere: otherwise, despite all the virtues and all the attraction of the tenderness which characterizes the gospel, the doctrine of the beatitudes, and of the Cross would long since have given place to some other, more winning, creed—and more particularly to some form of humanism or belief in purely earthly values.

Whatever the merits of other religions, it remains an undeniable fact—explain it how one will—that the most ardent and most massive blaze of collective love that has ever appeared in the world burns here and now in the heart of the Church of God.

◆ Teilhard de Chardin, Pierre, *Hymn of the Universe*. New York: Harper & Row, 1965.

Martin Luther King Jr. (1929–1968)

The son of a prominent black Baptist pastor in Atlanta, Martin Luther King Jr. studied at Morehouse College, Crozer Theological Seminary, and Boston University (Ph.D.) before becoming the pastor of the Drexler Avenue Baptist Church in Montgomery, Alabama. He vaulted into national prominence when he led the successful Montgomery bus boycott (1955–1956), which sought to end racial segregation on the city's public transportation. In 1957 King helped organize the Southern Christian Leadership Conference (SCLC), which rapidly became one of the foremost civil rights groups in the country. Most of its leaders were, like King, black Baptist ministers.

King's was the most important Christian voice in the drive for civil rights since World War II. His prestige was at its height in the early and mid-1960s. He keynoted the massive march on Washington in August 1963 with his moving "I have a dream" speech, and he helped organize the well-publicized Selma-to-Montgomery march in the spring of 1965. The first of those events provided major support for the Civil Rights Act of 1964, the second for the Voter Registration Act of 1965. King was awarded the Nobel Peace Prize in 1964.

Toward the end of his life, King's influence was somewhat in decline. His excursions into the North (Chicago, 1966, for example) cost him the support of those who saw civil rights as a strictly southern problem. His criticism of the Vietnam War angered other Americans. He was caught in the ideological crossfire caused by the rioting in American cities. Some whites held King responsible for those outbursts because of his promotion of black civil rights. Some blacks felt King betrayed their cause by continuing to repudiate the use of violence to attain racial justice. During the 1950s and 1960s King was a living example on American television screens of black preaching at its best. His speeches and writings drew heavily on the vocabulary provided by the rich reservoirs of black Christian history. His ideology was constructed on an evangelical realism about the nature of human evil and a scriptural defense of nonviolence ("love your enemies"). In classic black fashion he made little distinction between spiritual and social problems involved in the civil rights struggle.

King's books include *Stride Toward Freedom* (1958) and *Where Do We Go from Here: Chaos or Community?* (1967). It was often hard to tell where the Christian substratum of his thought left off and the superstructure of his social theory began. Other influences on his thinking were the pacifism of Gandhi, the civil disobedience of Thoreau, the philosophical idealism he had studied at Boston University, and the American public faith in democratic equality.

The chapters of *Strength to Love* are sermons preached by King at the Dexter Avenue Baptist Church of Montgomery, Alabama, and at Ebenezer Baptist Church of Atlanta, Georgia. They date from the days of the Montgomery bus boycott and after. Some were written while the author was in Georgia jails.

King writes in his preface:

> We live in a day of grave crisis. The sermons in this volume have the present crisis as their background. . . . In these sermons I have sought to bring the Christian message to bear on the social evils that cloud our day and the personal witness and discipline required.

Most of the fifteen chapters of *Strength to Love* are given a scriptural epigram. For example: (1) "'A tough mind and a tender heart'—Be ye therefore wise as serpents, and harmless as doves (Matthew 10:16)"; (2) "'Transformed nonconformist'— Be not conformed to this world: but be ye transformed by the renewing of your mind (Romans 12:2)"; (3) "'On being a good neighbor'—And who is my neighbor? (Luke 10:29)"; (8) "'The death of evil upon the seashore'—And Israel saw the Egyptians dead upon the sea shore (Exodus 14:30)"; (9) "'Shattered dreams'—Whensoever I take my journey into Spain, I will come to you (Romans 15:24)."

Coretta Scott King writes in her foreword to *Strength to Love:*

> If there is one book Martin Luther King Jr. has written that people consistently tell me has changed their lives, it is *Strength to Love.* I believe it is because this book best explains the central element of Martin Luther King Jr.'s philosophy of nonviolence: His belief in a divine, loving presence that binds all life. . . . Just as [he] sought the integration of the eternal and the temporal, he sought the integration of the spiritual and the intellectual. In the sermon "Love in action" he preached that "one day we will learn that the heart can never be totally right if the head is totally wrong. Only through the bringing together of head and heart—intelligence and goodness—shall man rise to a fulfillment of his true nature."

◆ King, Martin Luther, Jr. *Strength to Love.* Philadelphia: Fortress Press, 1986.

.... *Markings* 1964
Dag Hammarskjöld (1905–1961)

Dag Hammarskjöld was a Swedish monetary expert and statesman who served as the second secretary-general of the United Nations from 1953–1961. The son of a Swedish prime

minister, he studied law and economics at the universities of
Uppsala and Stockholm and taught for three years. He became
secretary and then chairman of the board of governors of the
Bank of Sweden and was undersecretary of the Swedish depart-
ment of finance from 1936 to 1945. He entered the Swedish civil
service in 1946.

In 1951 Hammarskjöld joined the Swedish delegation to the
United Nations and became its chairman in 1952. In 1953, he
was elected the UN's secretary-general. As such he applied his
moral authority and sensitivity to work for international peace.
In 1956 he worked to resolve the Suez crisis and in 1958 the
crisis in Lebanon and Jordan. In 1960 a crisis erupted in the
Congo, and Hammarskjöld, under protest from the USSR, sent
a UN peacemaking force into that country.

Hammarskjöld was killed in a plane crash while flying to
Katanga on a peace mission to negotiate a cease-fire between
the United Nations and Katanga forces. In 1961 he was posthumously awarded the Nobel Peace Prize.

Markings is a most unusual devotional book—the diary of a
prominent diplomat, not written for the public, yet posthumously
published with the author's permission. In his forward to the
book, the poet W. H. Auden writes:

> A reader of *Markings* may well be surprised by what it
> does not contain—that Dag Hammarskjöld should not
> make a single direct reference to his career as an interna-
> tional civil servant, to the persons he met, or the historical
> events of his time in which he played an important role. . . .

Markings contains intensely personal reflections, notes, say-
ings, and poems that describe the author's "longest journey . . .
the journey inwards." It is not a journal as such, nor a standard
autobiography; it is not teaching either. But *Markings* is an
invitation by example into a life of careful contemplation of one's

God, one's life, and one's service in this world. Hammarskjöld described the manuscript as a "sort of white book concerning my negotiations with myself and with God." The first entry is a poem written about 1925; the book ends with a poem he wrote only a few weeks before his death.

Here is a poem by Dag Hammarskjöld from November 26, 1960:

> *The moon was caught in the branches:*
> *Bound by its vow,*
> *My heart was heavy.*
>
> *Naked against the night*
> *The trees slept. "Nevertheless,*
> *Not as I will . . ."*
>
> *The burden remained mine:*
> *They could not hear my call,*
> *And all was silence.*
>
> *Soon, now, the torches, the kiss:*
> *Soon the gray of dawn*
> *In the Judgment Hall.*
>
> *What will their love help there?*
> *There, the question is only*
> *If I love them.*

◆ Hammarskjöld, Dag, *Markings*. Translated by W. H. Auden and Leif Sjöberg. New York: Alfred A. Knopf, 1964.

. . . . *Biography of James Hudson Taylor* **1965**
   Dr. and Mrs. Howard Taylor

The original full standard biography of James Hudson Taylor (1832–1905), founder of the China Inland Mission, is contained in two volumes: *Early Years—The Growth of a Soul* (1911) and *China Inland Mission—The Growth of a Work of God* (1918). These have seen at least seventeen editions and appeared in six European languages. An abridgment of this biography in one volume, *Biography of James Hudson Taylor,* was published in 1965 for the centennial year of the China Inland Mission (now known as Overseas Missionary Fellowship). Taylor's life was so full of incident and meaning that this shortened version of his biography runs over five hundred pages in the paperback edition.

Hudson Taylor is the archetype missionary hero. Born into a Methodist family in Barnsley, Yorkshire, England, Taylor was influenced spiritually by his parents and grandparents (who had received John Wesley as a house guest). His father, a pharmacist, was concerned that the gospel would reach the Chinese people. When he was about five years of age, Hudson Taylor precociously said he would like to be a missionary to China.

But first, the young man became skeptical and worldly. At fifteen he entered a local bank and worked as a junior clerk— well adjusted and popular. He left the bank in 1848 to work in his father's shop. The next year, while reading a tract on the finished work of Christ, Taylor felt that he finally understood what Christ had done for him. The same year, at age seventeen, he felt the Lord's call to missionary work in China.

In preparation for this work, Taylor began to learn Mandarin Chinese by comparing the Mandarin translation of the Gospel of Luke with its English version. He also turned from training in pharmacy to medicine. Then, as he was studying in London, he became convinced that he would not be prepared for work in China without depending on God for everything. This is one of several inspiring devotional themes that run through Taylor's biography.

Taylor was not above placing himself in situations that

demanded that God meet his financial needs. Once as he was
ministering to the poor, a man asked him to pray for his wife,
who was near death. Taylor went to the man's house. There he
saw starving children and their sick mother with an infant moan-
ing at her side. Not only did he pray, he also gave the man his
last coin to be used to save the woman's life. Later that day a
package was delivered to Taylor. In it was money. This and
other experiences emboldened Taylor to depend solely on God
for his needs.

In 1853 Taylor sailed for China in association with the Chinese
Evangelization Society. But no one met him at his arrival in
Shanghai, a huge city occupied by rebels. So the new missionary
associated himself with other Christian workers in the area, studied Chinese, and began to preach the gospel. Soon he desired to
evangelize inland areas of China. Missionaries at that time
restricted their work to certain coastal cities for political reasons.
Also, it was illegal for foreigners to travel inland.

Still, Taylor and a fellow worker took short excursions
inland, taking turns speaking the gospel and distributing tracts
and Scripture portions. This was dangerous work. Soon Taylor
adopted native dress that did much to win the respect of the
Chinese, although it alienated him from his fellow missionaries.

In one of his early letters home he wrote:

> At home, you can never know what it is to be absolutely
> alone, amidst thousands, everyone looking on you with curi-
> osity, with contempt, with suspicion, or with dislike. Thus
> to learn what it is to be despised and rejected of men . . . and
> then to have the love of Jesus applied to your heart by the
> Holy Spirit . . . this is precious, this is worth coming for.

Hudson Taylor was working in Ningpo in 1856 when he
decided to sever his connection with the Chinese Evangelization
Society. The society had been operating on borrowed money.

Taylor believed that a Christian should "owe no man anything." He also felt that if a work lacked funds, God must no longer support it.

Independent of all but God, Taylor married Maria Dyer in 1858, and in 1859 he took charge of the London Mission Hospital in Ningpo. Failing health forced his resignation from the hospital within a year, but its work had prospered in every way under his direction.

By 1860 Taylor was in his late twenties. Though his work in the gospel was growing, his health was broken, and he returned to England. Doctors assured him that it would be years before he would return to China, if at all. So Hudson Taylor posted a large map of China on his wall and prayed that workers be prepared to go there. He himself worked on a revision of the New Testament in colloquial Ningpo Chinese.

As new missionaries emerged and set out for China, Taylor formed an agency that was especially suited for the work of the gospel in interior China—the China Inland Mission was dependent only upon God for all financial needs. This meant that there were no private or public solicitations for financial support, nor were collections made in meetings when Taylor spoke. But there was much prayer. A reader of this biography will be strengthened in this spiritual exercise.

In 1865 Taylor petitioned God for twenty-four fellow workers—two for each of the evangelized inland provinces and two for Mongolia. In 1866 he and Maria sailed with a group of new missionaries for China. From Ningpo and Hangchow, the work spread southward to the province of Chekaing. Ten years later it was spreading north to Kiangsu, west to Anhwei, and southwest to Kiangsi. In 1870, shortly after the death of an infant son to cholera, Maria also died of the disease.

The pioneering work of the China Inland Mission spread throughout the whole interior of China. Christians from many countries and denominations put aside their differences to join the ranks of the China Inland Mission. By the end of the century, half of the evangelical missionaries in China were fellow workers with Hudson Taylor. By 1895 the Mission had 641 missionaries and 462 Chinese helpers at 260 stations. During the Boxer Rebellion of 1900, 56 of these missionaries were martyred, and hundreds of Chinese Christians were killed. Taylor withdrew from the work in 1901 and died in Changsha in 1905.

Trust and love of God and steadfast prayer are inspiring devotional lessons one may learn from the life of Hudson Taylor. A third is a foundation for all—his profound love of the Bible, for which he seems to always have had time, no matter how exhausting the work.

- ◆ Taylor, Howard. *Biography of James Hudson Taylor.* London: Hodder & Stoughton, 1997.

- ◆ Steer, James. *J. Hudson Taylor: A Man in Christ.* Singapore: OMF Books, 1993.

- ◆ Taylor, Hudson. *Union and Communion.* Darlington, England: Evangelical Press, 1996.

▸ . . . . *Contemplative Prayer* **1969**
   Thomas Merton (1915–1968)

Thomas Merton was born in Prades, France, on January 31, 1915, in the foothills of the Pyrenees Mountains, not far from the Spanish border. His father, Owen Merton, a New Zealander, was a landscape painter. His mother, Ruth Jenkins, an American Quaker, had studied interior design.

After a year at Cambridge University in England, he went to the United States to live with his maternal grandparents, who had funded his education. Merton then enrolled in Columbia

University where his teachers included Mark Van Doren and Daniel C. Walsh. He entered the Catholic church after a dramatic conversion experience in 1938. Upon completion of his masters degree (thesis: "On Nature and Art in William Blake"), he taught at Columbia University Extension and St. Bonaventure's University in Olean, upstate New York. On December 10, 1941, he entered the Trappist monastic community of the Abbey of Gethsemani, Kentucky.

In his autobiography, *The Seven Storey Mountain* (1948), the young monk wrote of the profound spiritual experiences that prompted him to join the monastery. This soon became a best-seller and is now a classic of Christian literature. This book made Merton a well-known religious figure and established writer. A sequel autobiography, *The Sign of Jonas* (1952), provides a vivid description of life in a Trappist monastery.

Merton wrote prolifically on a vast range of topics, including the contemplative life, prayer, and biography. He also addressed controversial issues such as social problems and Christian responsibility, including race relations, violence, nuclear war, economic injustice, and ecumenical concerns, and interpreted the religions of Asia to Christians.

Thomas Merton is best known for his personal mysticism as expressed in his poems: *Thirty Poems* (1944), a volume that was written in "the first flush of his conversion"; *Figs for an Apocalypse* (1947) and *Tears of the Blind Lions* (1949), two volumes that express his Catholic spirituality in vigorous verse. He died in an accident in Bangkok, Thailand, while attending a meeting of religious leaders in 1968.

Contemplative Prayer is the last book Merton wrote before his death. It was written primarily for fellow monks who might often be alone (even if they were isolated out of choice, as in the Trappist order). But it contains priceless wisdom for all Christians who long to go deeper in the spiritual life. Here the author comments on texts from Scripture and from writers in the tradition of Western contemplative spirituality—from John of the Cross to Eastern desert monasticism—shifting them to the present and applying them to modern problems. Merton declares that even the most isolated Christian is still part of a larger community, manifest in the universal church. Merton writes:

> The Christian is never merely an isolated individual. He is a member of the praising community, the People of God. *Alleluia* is the victorious acclamation of the Risen Savior. . . . We acclaim God as members of a community that has been blessed and saved and is traveling to meet him as he comes in his promised Advent.

Merton continues:

> One cannot begin to face the real difficulties of the life of prayer and meditation unless one is first perfectly content to be a beginner and really experience himself as one who knows little or nothing and has a desperate need to learn the bare rudiments. Those who think they "know" from the beginning will never, in fact, come to know anything.

♦ Merton, Thomas. *Contemplative Prayer.* New York: Doubleday & Co., 1992.

.... *True Spirituality* 1971
Francis A. Schaeffer 1912–1984

The evangelical missionary, philosopher, author, and lecturer Francis August Schaeffer was born in Philadelphia into a Lutheran family but became an agnostic during his teen years. It was while he was studying engineering at Drexel Institute that he became a believer in Christ.

In 1935 he completed his college work *magna cum laude* at

Hampden Sidney College, Virginia, a southern Presbyterian school. There he received his bachelor of arts degree. Also in 1935 Schaeffer married Edith Seville. Schaeffer then attended Westminster Theological Seminary in Philadelphia, studying under Cornelius van Til, a Reformed apologist from the Netherlands, and finished his training at Faith Theological Seminary, Wilmington, Delaware, receiving his bachelor of divinity degree in 1938.

Schaeffer was the first ordained minister of the Bible Presbyterian Church and went on to pastor other churches in Pennsylvania and St. Louis, Missouri. In 1971 he was awarded a doctor of laws degree by Gordon College, Wenham, Massachusetts.

The Schaeffer family was moved to Switzerland by the Independent Board for Presbyterian Foreign Missions in 1948. There Francis and Edith became vitally concerned for the youth from all nations. As a result, in 1955, they founded an international study and ministry community in the Swiss Alps at Huemoz, which they called *L'Abri* (shelter). Students from all cultures and beliefs were welcomed at L'Abri. There they discussed secular culture and ideas. Through study and prayer, many of the thousands of people who visited at L'Abri became Christians. The story of the founding and development of the L'Abri community is told by Edith Schaeffer in *L'Abri* (1969). L'Abri gradually became known throughout Europe and beyond as "a place where one could discuss the great twentieth-century questions quite openly." Eventually L'Abri had centers in Milan, London, Amsterdam, and Rochester, Minnesota.

Most of Schaeffer's books grew out of lectures and discussions at L'Abri Fellowship. His ministry gained worldwide recognition through the distribution of these books, which include *The God Who Is There* (1968); *Escape from Reason* (1968); *Pollution and the Death of Man* (1970); *The Church at the End of the Twentieth Century* (1970); *True Spirituality*

(1971); *He Is There and He Is Not Silent* (1972); *How Should We Then Live: The Rise and Decline of Western Thought and Culture* (1976). In his books as well as in his lectures, Schaeffer sought to relate biblical Christianity to philosophical questions and contemporary culture.

Schaeffer is described as a theologian, a philosopher, and a cultural historian. But he viewed himself primarily as an evangelist. He defined his task as "first of all, giving honest answers to honest questions to get the blocks out of the way so that people will listen to the gospel as a viable alternative, and then secondly, showing them what Christianity means across the whole spectrum of life." For Schaeffer, this meant confronting the people of the twentieth century with the results of humanism ("man's starting with himself alone") and proposing the Christian alternative to answer the questions humanism leaves unanswered.

Schaeffer attributed much of today's social ills to the teaching of the philosopher Hegel, who promoted the thought that truth is relative and not absolute. Schaeffer's writings, twenty-four books in all, describe the disastrous political and moral consequences of adopting Hegel's view and contends that the only remedy for our world is a return to biblical absolutes.

In 1979 Schaeffer toured the United States with Dr. C. Everett Koop (later surgeon general of the United States during the Reagan administration). They lectured and screened a film entitled *Whatever Happened to the Human Race?* The film contends that secular humanism has replaced God's laws as the basis of contemporary ethics.

In *True Spirituality* Schaeffer places Christ's redemptive power at the center of the Christian life. The book is a devotional commentary loosely structured on the book of Romans, which characterizes true spirituality by the results of the redemption: freedom from sin, emotional and spiritual wholeness, and unity with others. For Schaeffer, the essence of this life is not found in living by an external set of rules but rather living by faith as a holy sacrifice unto God.

True Spirituality is composed of thirteen chapters divided into two sections. The seven chapters of Section 1 ("Freedom Now from the Bonds of Sin") are subdivided into three sections: "Basic Considerations of True Spirituality," "Biblical Unity and True Spirituality," and "Moment by Moment Practice of True Spirituality." Section 2 ("Freedom Now from the Results of the Bonds of Sin") contains six chapters that are subdivided into two groups: "Man's Separation from Himself" and "Man's Separation from His Fellowman."

In his first chapter, "The Law and the Law of Love," Schaeffer writes: "When I speak of the Christian life, or freedom from the bonds of sin, or of true spirituality, . . . four points . . . are what the Bible says we should mean, and anything less than this is trifling with God—trifling with him who created the world, and trifling also with him who died on the cross." Schaeffer's four points are these:

1. The true Christian life, true spirituality, does not mean just that we have been born again and are going to heaven. It must begin there, but it means much more than that.
2. True spirituality is not just a desire to get rid of taboos in order to live an easier and a looser life. Our desire must be for a deeper life. And when we begin to think of this, the Bible presents to us the whole of the Ten Commandments and the whole of the law of love.
3. True spirituality, the true Christian life, is not just outward but also inward—it is not to covet against God and people.
4. But true spirituality is even more than this: It is positive— positive in inward reality and then positive in outward results. It is not just that we are dead to certain things, but we are to love God, we are to be alive to him, we are to be

in communion with him *in this present moment of history.* And we are to love others, to be alive to others as people, and to be in communication on a true personal level with them *in this present moment of history.*

"The question before us," says Francis Schaeffer in the first sentence of *True Spirituality,* "is what the Christian life, true spirituality, really is, and how it may be lived in a twentieth-century setting." The thirteen chapters of *True Spirituality* are his answer.

◆ Schaeffer, Francis A. *True Spirituality.* Wheaton, Ill.: Tyndale House Publishers, 1991.

.... *The Wounded Healer* **1972**
Henri Nouwen (1932–1996)

Henri Nouwen was an author, Catholic priest, and psychologist. Ordained in 1957, Nouwen pursued advanced studies in the field of psychology, and from 1964 through 1981 he held positions at the Menninger Clinic, Notre Dame University, the University of Nijmegen, and Yale University.

Nouwen's books include *Making All Things New: An Invitation to the Spiritual Life* (1981), *The Genesee Diary: Report from a Trappist Monastery* (1985), and *The Road to Daybreak: A Spiritual Journey* (1988).

About 1980 Nouwen began to pursue what he called "the descending way of Christ" and spent six months in Bolivia and Peru as a missionary to the poor. After time spent in Mexico, Nicaragua, and Honduras, he returned to the United States to lecture on his experiences there. In 1986 Nouwen began to serve in the L'Arche communities and did so until his death.

Founded by the Canadian Jean Vanier, L'Arche is an international network of communities where people with developmental disabilities and their friends live together. There Nouwen, the celebrated and much translated author, found a place where his reputation meant nothing—many members of the community could not read. There he could count among his friends Adam Arnett (1961–1996), a man who never spoke a word. Perhaps Nouwen's "descending way of Christ" led him to L'Arche. Certainly L'Arche gave Nouwen an ideal opportunity to practice the ministry of a wounded healer.

Nouwen's book *The Wounded Healer* begins with a question:

> What does it mean to be a minister in our contemporary society? This question has been raised during the last few years by many men and women who want to be of service, but who find the familiar ways crumbling and themselves stripped of their traditional protections.

The following chapters are an attempt to respond to this question.

Nouwen combines case studies of ministry with stories from diverse cultures and religious traditions to describe a new model for ministry. He combines cultural analysis and psychological and religious insights to form a balanced theology of Christian service. The book is composed of four chapters in which the author describes the conditions of a suffering world, a suffering generation, a suffering person, and a suffering minister.

The author declares that a minister can recognize contemporary suffering and so identify that suffering in his own heart. This is the beginning of his service. In the image of Christ, the minister goes beyond professional position to become open to those with similar suffering. In other words, despite one's own weakness, a minister can participate in others' healing. Here Nouwen explains this in terms of loneliness:

So we see how loneliness is the minister's wound not only because he shares in the human condition but also because of the unique predicament of his profession. It is this wound which he is called to bind with more care and attention than others usually do. For a deep understanding of his own pain makes it possible for him to convert his weakness into strength and to offer his own experience as a source of healing to those who are often lost in the darkness of their own misunderstood sufferings. . . . Loneliness is a very painful wound which is easily subject to denial and neglect. But once the pain is accepted and understood, a denial is no longer necessary, and ministry can become a healing service.

Here is a book to excite the meditation, prayer, and action of anyone who desires to effectively serve God in this world.

♦ Nouwen, Henri J. M. *The Wounded Healer.* New York: Image Books, 1979.

. . . . *Knowing God* 1973
J. I. Packer (b. 1926)

James Innell Packer was born July 22, 1926, in Twyning, Gloucestershire, England, and educated at Corpus Christi College, Oxford. There he received a B.A. in 1948 and both his M.A. and Ph.D. in 1954.

As he was finishing his studies, J. I. Packer became an Anglican clergyman, serving as assistant curate in Birmingham, England, from 1952 to 1954. Then he began his academic career as tutor at Tyndale Hall, Bristol, England, 1955–61. From 1961 to 1969 Packer worked as librarian and, later, warden at Latimer House, Oxford. He was then appointed principal at Tyndale Hall,

1970–1971, and then associate principal at Trinity College, Bristol, 1971–1979. Packer is currently Sangwoo Youtong Chee Professor of Theology at Regent College, Vancouver, British Columbia.

Dr. Packer has published more than fifteen books since 1958, when he completed *Fundamentalism and the Word of God.* A prolific writer, his well-known books are *Knowing God, The Sovereignty of God,* and *The Quest for Godliness.* His recent publications include *Knowing and Doing the Will of God, Great Grace,* and *Great Joy.* Packer has preached and lectured widely in Great Britain and America and is a frequent contributor to theological periodicals. He is also a senior editor and visiting scholar with *Christianity Today* magazine.

Published in fourteen languages, *Knowing God* is a series of studies first published in *Evangelical Magazine.* Packer writes, "The conviction behind the book is that ignorance of God—ignorance of both his ways and of the practice of communion with him—lies at the root of much of the church's weakness today." The sources of such ignorance are traced to two trends: (1) Christian minds have been conformed to the modern spirit, and (2) Christian minds have been confused by the modern skepticism.

The twenty-two chapters of *Knowing God* are subdivided into three sections: "Know the Lord," "Behold Your God!" and "If God Be For Us . . ." In his introduction to the book Packer quotes Jeremiah 6:16: "Stand ye in the ways, and see, and ask for the old paths, where is the good way, and walk therein, and ye shall find rest for your souls" (KJV). He continues:

> Such is the invitation which this book issues. It is not a critique of new paths, except indirectly, but rather a straightforward recall to old ones, on the ground that "the good way" is still what it used to be. . . . "[S]ince we have the same spirit of faith as he had who wrote, 'I believed, and so I

spoke,' we too believe, and so we speak" (2 Corinthians 4:13 RSV)—and if what is written here helps anyone in the way that the meditations behind the writing helped me, the work will have been abundantly worth while.

The book is a view of who God is. This includes God's unchanging nature, majesty, wisdom, love, grace, judgment, wrath, goodness, and jealousy. But Packer makes clear the difference between knowing about God and knowing God, yet also states with insight, "What matters supremely, therefore, is not, in the last analysis, the fact that I know God, but the larger fact which underlies it—the fact that he knows me."

◆ Packer, J. I. *Knowing God.* Downers Grove, Ill.: InterVarsity Press, 1993.

.... *Letters to Scattered Pilgrims* **1979**
Elizabeth O'Connor (1921–1998)

Elizabeth O'Connor may be considered the amanuensis of a community, the Church of the Saviour in Washington, D.C., which was founded in 1947. O'Connor was an early member who later joined the church staff and began to chronicle the Lord's remarkable work there. Her books include *Journey Inward, Journey Outward; Cry Pain, Cry Hope: A Guide to the Dimensions of Call; Eighth Day of Creation: Discovering Your Gifts; Call to Commitment: An Attempt to Embody the Essence of Church;* and *Letters to Scattered Pilgrims.*

Although the Church of the Saviour had a pastor, it was and is organized around the concept of the priesthood of all believers— "But you are a chosen race, a royal priesthood, a consecrated nation, a people set apart . . ." (1 Peter 2:9, TJB). By 1975 the church had twenty-five small mission groups made up of five to twelve persons. Each group was functioning effectively, but the church found that communication was breaking down between its members. So, instead of taking the traditional way of adding more professional staff to meet the need, the Church of the Saviour decided to again trust lay persons to be ministers. It reformed itself into six new church communities.

In her preface to *Letters to Scattered Pilgrims,* O'Connor tells of this time:

> As in every passage, it was a time of crisis, carrying the possibility of death or of new life. We might have lost heart and returned to the known, only as with the Israelites there was no one to lead the way back, no Moses figure with the word of Yahweh in his mouth. The old had been forever lost, and the new did not yet exist in any important way. It was a time of anger, tears, complaints and disillusionment. It was a time of hoping, of planting seeds, forgiving, trusting, asking, and watching until the hidden light in each one's life became by day "the form of a pillar of cloud," and by night "the form of a pillar of fire" (Exodus 13:21, TJB).

O'Connor wrote letters to the six new communities—to the Dayspring Church, the Dunamis Vocations Church, the Eighth Day Church, the Jubilee Church, the Potter's House Church, and the Seekers Church. The letters make up the eleven chapters of *Letters to Pilgrims:*

1. "On Having Time for Reflection"
2. "On Money"
3. "More on Money"
4. "On Keeping a Journal"
5. "On the Journal and Group Life"
6. "On Our Multidimensional Nature"
7. "On Our Historical Center"

8. "On Our Intellectual Center"
9. "On Our Emotional Center"
10. "On Our Moving Center"
11. "On Children in the Wilderness"

Here is a portion of O'Connor's writing about money:

> None of us has to be an accountant to know what 10 percent of a gross income is, but each of us has to be a person on his knees before God if we are to understand our commitment to proportionate giving.

Proportionate to what? Proportionate to the accumulated wealth of one's family? Proportionate to one's income and the demands upon it, which vary from family to family? Proportionate to one's sense of security and the degree of anxiety with which one lives? Proportionate to the keenness of our awareness of justice and of God's ownership of all wealth? Proportionate to our sense of stewardship for those who follow after us? And so, and so forth. The answer, of course, is in proportion to all of these things.

These chapters are not only a gift to a particular community, but, as Elizabeth O'Connor described, they are gathered together "for whatever help they may be for pilgrim persons all over the world, who are sensing God's call to the building of a more caring and just society."

◆ O'Connor, Elizabeth. *Letters to Scattered Pilgrims.* New York: Harper & Row, 1979.

.... *The Oxford Book of Prayer* **1985**
George Appleton, general editor

The Oxford Book of Prayer is a compilation of over eleven hundred prayers. Both traditional and modern, its sources extend from the Bible, to the saints and mystics of the past, to the *Book of Common Prayer,* to a Ghanaian fisherman's prayer. The editor, Anglican bishop George Appleton, writes in his introduction to *The Oxford Book of Prayer:*

> When this anthology was conceived the compilers hardly realized the immensity of the task they had undertaken. After five years of labor they are almost moved to pray with the prophet Jeremiah, "Lord, thou hast deceived me." You did not make clear the travail and labor which would be needed! With the completion of the task, all realize how imperfectly it has been done, yet they offer it to God and to their fellow men, in the hope that it will witness to the reality of God, to the spiritual nature with which he has endowed man, and will deepen the interior life of those into whose hands the book may come.

Because this book draws prayers from so many sources, many of which are unavailable to the average reader, and because such literature will surely, as Appleton says, "deepen the interior life" of the reader, we include it here. The selections have both spiritual quality and literary merit. The prayers do not only speak; they are eloquent.

Appleton and a group of about a dozen people representing the main Christian traditions compiled the book and arranged it in six sections: "Prayers of Adoration," "Prayers from the Scripture," "Prayers of Christians, Personal and Occasional," "Prayers of the Church," "Prayers of Listening," and "Prayers of Other Traditions of Faith." The anthology includes a subject index to guide the reader to prayers for particular occasions, as well as an index of authors and sources. It serves as a source for browsing, structured prayer, private meditation, or public worship.

The center of the book is "Prayers of Christians, Personal and

Occasional," whose subsections are arranged in terms of phrases from the Lord's Prayer as follows:

> Our Father (Dependence) who art in heaven (Affirmation), Hallowed be thy name (Blessing and Thanksgiving). Thy Kingdom come (Longing; Seeking; Doing; Serving; Peace). Thy will be done (Dedication; Obedience), on earth as it is in heaven (Guidance; Acceptance). Give us this day our daily bread (Daily; Graces). And forgive us our trespasses (Penitence), as we forgive them that trespass against us (Relationships). And lead us not into temptation (Right Living); but deliver us from evil (Protection; Suffering; Compassion). For thine is the kingdom (Devotion; Contemplation; Gifts of the Spirit; Sacraments), the power, and the glory, for ever and ever (Death and eternity; The Virgin, Martyrs, and Saints; Blessings). Amen.

Christians pray. It is the heart of devotion to God. It is the expression of a basic attitude of dependence and humility towards the Creator. *The Oxford Book of Prayer* records the prayers of the famous and the common, some of whom may view God very differently than the reader. But through prayerful reading, one may find a deeper understanding not only of God but of fellow believers.

◆ Appleton, George, ed. *The Oxford Book of Prayer.* New York: Oxford University Press, 1989.

TIMELINE

c. 30	Jesus' crucifixion and resurrection
70	The destruction of the temple in Jerusalem
132	Bar Kokhba leads a revolt in Palestine
324	Constantine secures his rule over the Roman Empire
395	The Roman Empire is divided into East and West
410	Barbarians attack Rome
c. 570	Muhammad is born
800	Charlemagne is crowned emperor of the Holy Roman Empire
1054	The Church officially splits, separating Roman Catholicism from Eastern Orthodoxy
1066	William of Normandy conquers England
1095	The First Crusade
1215	The Magna Carta is drafted
c. 1348	Black Death spreads throughout Europe
c. 1450	Johannes Gutenberg invents his printing press
1492	Christopher Columbus arrives in the New World
1504	Michelangelo completes his sculpture of David
1517	Martin Luther nails his Ninety-Five Theses to the chapel door
1534	Henry VIII establishes the Church of England
1536	William Tyndale is strangled and burned at the stake
1543	Nicolaus Copernicus publishes *On the Revolutions of Heavenly Spheres*
1563	Council of Trent is adjourned
1616	William Shakespeare dies
1620	Pilgrims arrive in America
1640	The English Civil War
1769	James Watt invents the steam engine
1776	The American Revolution
1789	The French Revolution

1815   Napoleon Bonaparte is defeated at Waterloo
1848   Karl Marx publishes his *Communist Manifesto*
1859   Charles Darwin publishes *On the Origin of
Species by Means of Natural Selection*
1865   The American Civil War ends
1918   World War I ends
1929   The Great Depression begins in America
1945   World War II ends
1963   Civil Rights march in Washington, D.C.